MY MOTIVATIONAL
Print Handwriting & Numbers Workbook
For Beginners

By Dr. Denisha M Brown

MY MOTIVATIONAL
PRINT HANDWRITING & NUMBERS WORKBOOK

ISBN: 979-8-9858105-3-0

This Book Belongs To

_____

_____

Author's Message

Children are like sponges between the ages of 1-5 years old by soaking up information and new skills taught to them. They begin to develop their personality, self esteem, and confidence, which is essential to learning.

I am Dr. Denisha M. Brown, an educational leader and educational consultant. I specialized in Early Childhood Education and social emotional development of children. My professional and personal experiences have afforded me the opportunity to observe and research the importance of engaging students in fun educational activities that support phonics, reading, writing, and math development at an early age. Therefore, this workbook was developed to teach children from ages 1- 5 years old letter recognition, number recognition, writing, motivational words, and so much more.

This workbook was created with the goal to prepare young scholars with the tools he or she may need to begin their academic career in Pre-K or Kindergarten. I encourage you to use this workbook to guide your child to practice at their own pace. You will find that early support and exposure will help your child learn and store lessons that their brian will recall to become a dynamic scholar in the future. Let's work together to shape the minds of our future leaders while spreading positivity in the world!

Tell me how you enjoyed the book by leaving a review.
You may also follow us or tag us on all social media platforms using the handle: @Fan_EdServices.
Thank you for your purchase and enjoy!

Dr. Denisha M Brown

My Motivational Print Handwriting & Numbers Workbook was created for young beginners to learn letters and numbers.

The combination of letters and numbers in this workbook allows your child to work on line tracing practice, letter identification, number identification, writing, and counting. In addition, each alphabet has a motivational word that begins with the corresponding letter. The motivational words and phrases throughout the book can be used to increase the self-esteem and confidence of your child. Reciting affirmations also, provides a sense of reassurance when children are faced with difficult tasks or told something negative about themself, he or she can refer to the positive affirmation learned to deny any negative thoughts and believe the positive thoughts.

This workbook is organized in a way to set your child up for success before entering Pre-K or Kindergarten. The alphabets are organized by the stroke, which means letters with similar line strokes are grouped together. Additionally, the lowercase letter of each alphabet comes prior to the uppercase. The lowercase letters are seen more often in print when children read and write. Therefore, research suggests it is best to teach lowercase letters first, prior to uppercase letters.

I would like to thank you for your purchase and hope you and your child enjoy the endless possibilities of learning with this workbook. Please refer to the helpful suggestions listed below for any additional support on how to best use this resource . Be so kind and tell us how you enjoyed this book by leaving a review.
Don't forget to tag us @Fan_EdServices on all social media platforms.

Helpful Suggestions

1. Allow your child to practice handwriting skills at least 3 times a week. When your child becomes confident with tracing, move them on to writing on their own.

2. If your child struggles with writing letters with a writing utensil, try forming letters using shaving cream or sand in a tray. This will allow your child to feel the movement of different strokes for each letter. Visit our site FanEdServices.com to purchase a play sand tray kit.

3. Use a pencil gripper to assist with holding the pencil correctly.

4. Have your child complete the different activity pages such as coloring, identifying letters and numbers, practicing initial sounds of letters, line practice, and following one-step directions.

5. Have your child recite and memorize the positive affirmations on each activity page and tracing page. This will increase your child's self-esteem and confidence.

6. You can extend the affirmation practice by reciting them daily or writing them as notes to place in a lunch bag, on the mirror, or around your child's room.

7. Ask your child to find words or objects that start with a letter of practice and practice quantities, addition, and subtraction with the numbers learned.

8. Use the flashcards in the back of this workbook to practice letter and number identification and so much more. You may laminate the sheets prior to cutting out for lasting usage.

Parents, please read above.

Trace and color shapes.

CIRCLE

SQUARE

TRIANGLE

CRESCENT

ELLIPSE

RECTANGLE

PENTAGON

OCTAGON

HEPTAGON

HEART

POLYGON

DIAMOND

STAR

ARROW

QUATREFOIL

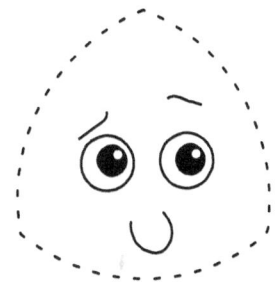
CURVILINEAR
TRIANGLE

Color and practice naming the shapes.

2-D Shapes

 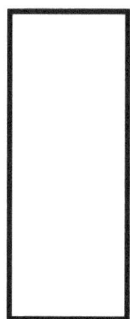 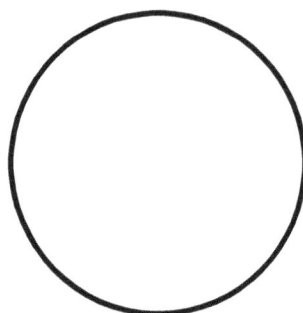 

Square   Rectangle   Circle   Oval

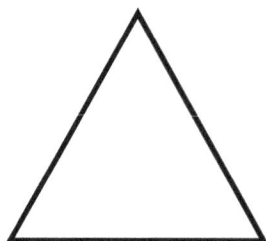 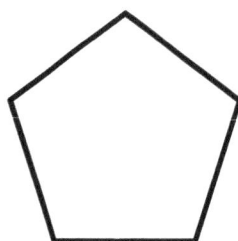 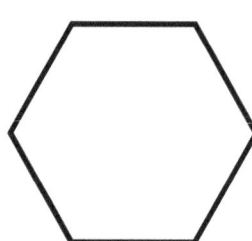 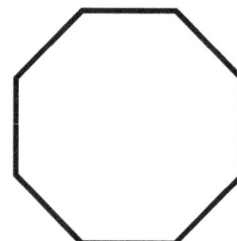

Triangle   Pentagon   Hexagon   Octagon

3-D Shapes

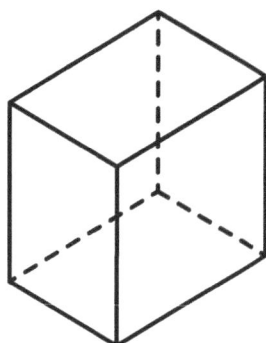 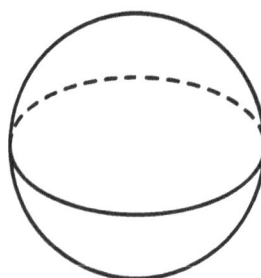 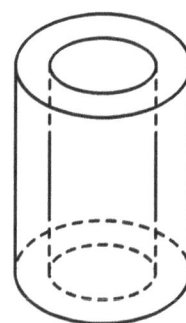

Cube   Sphere   Cylinder

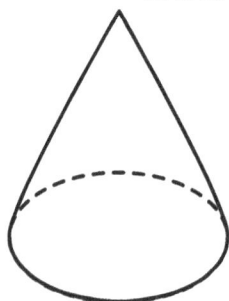 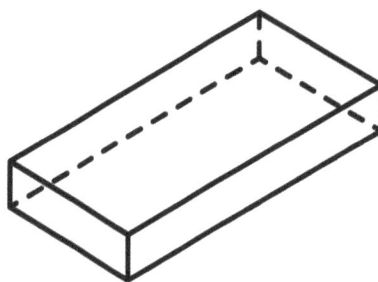 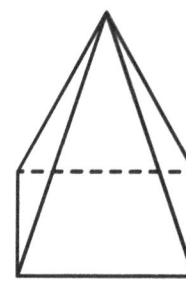

Cone   Rectangular Prism   Pyramid

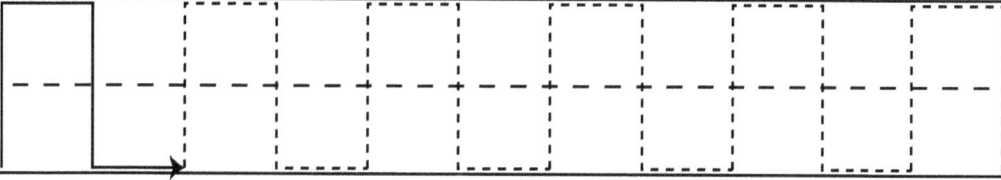

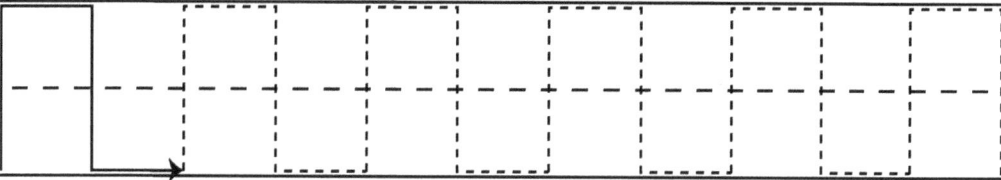

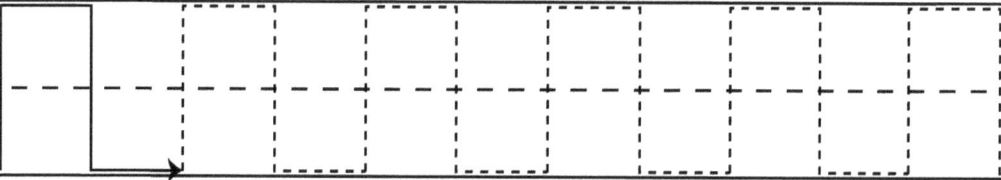

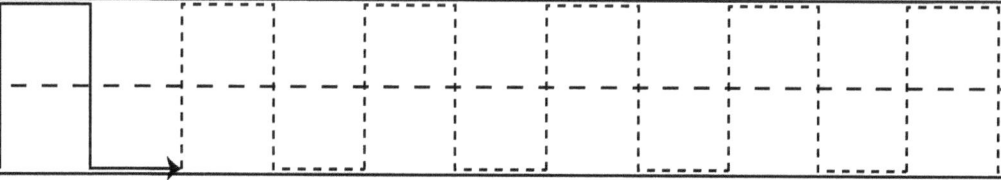

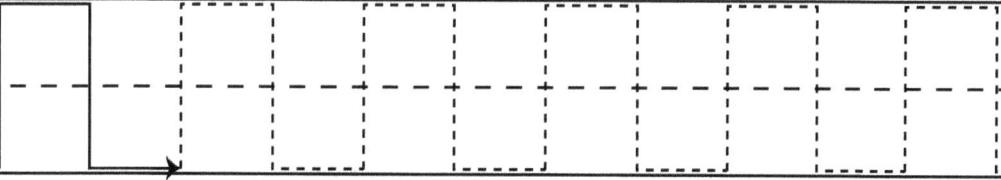

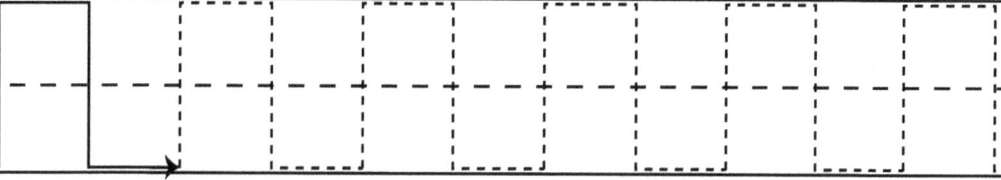

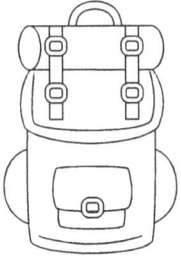

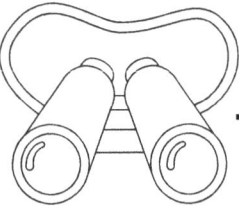

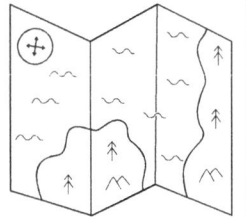

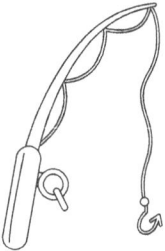

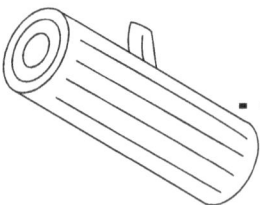

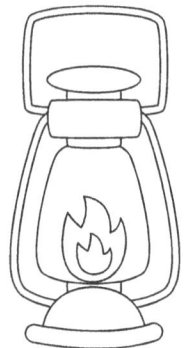

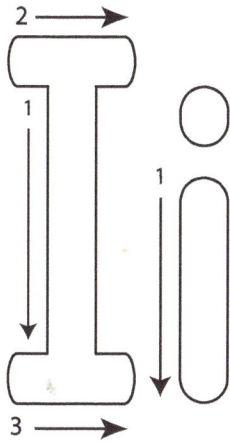

I i

iguana

Trace and write

i i i i i i i

i i i i i i i

I I I I I I

I I I I I I

Ii Ii Ii Ii Ii

Incredible   Incredible

Trace and Write.

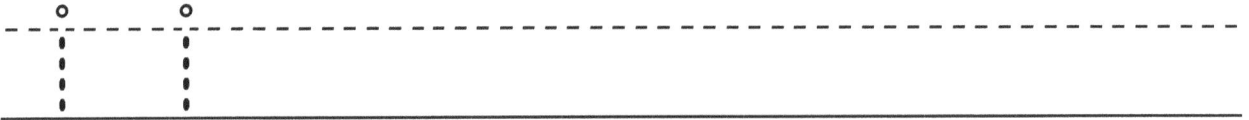

Practice writing a lowercase i.

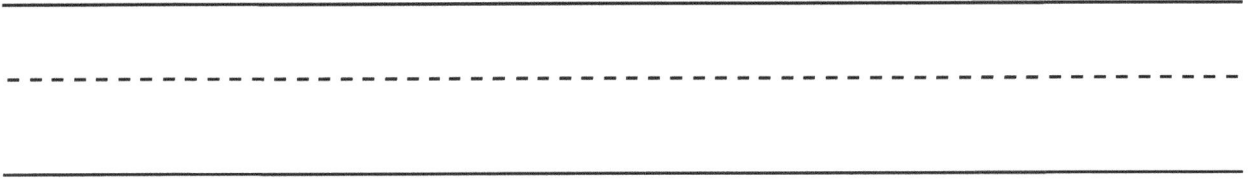

Trace and Write.

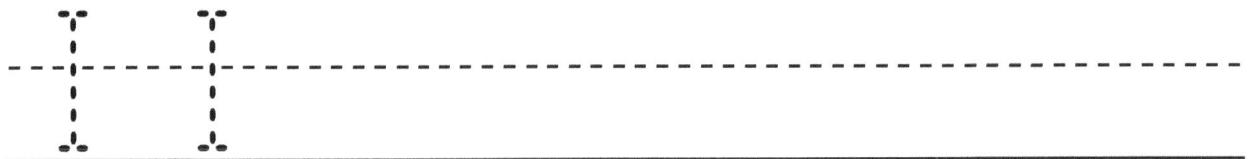

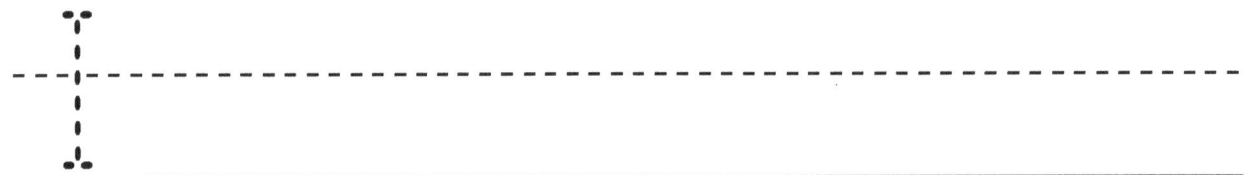

Practice writing an uppercase I.

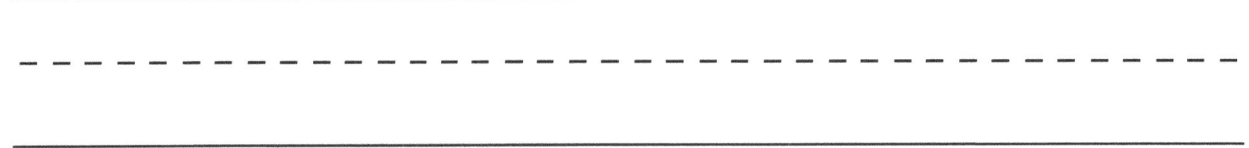

Trace.

I am incredible!

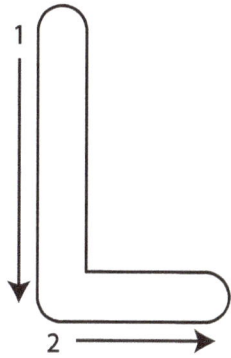

Ll

lamp

Trace and write

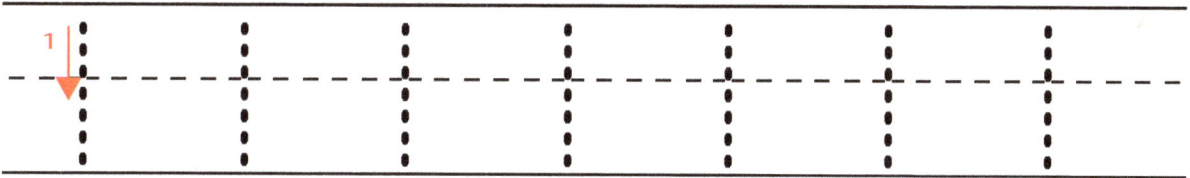

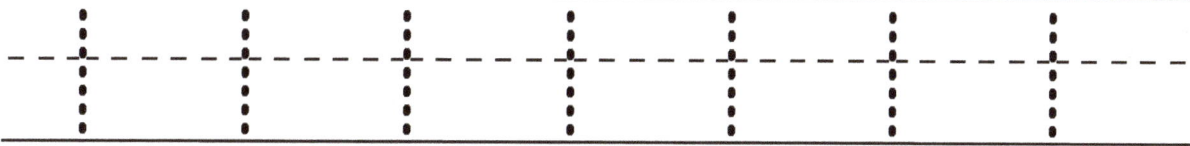

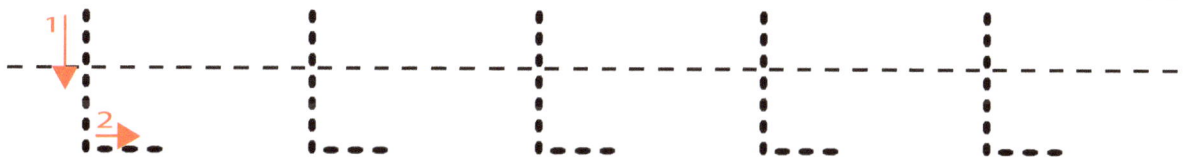

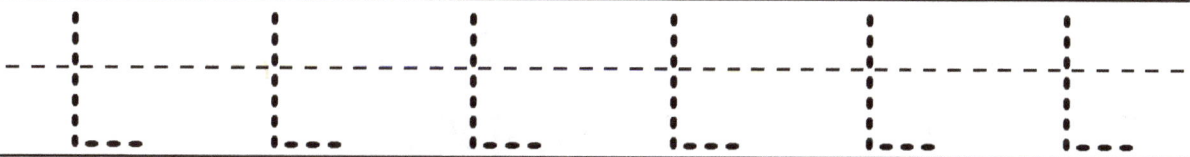

l l l l l l l

l l l l l l l

L L L L L

L L L L L L

Ll Ll Ll Ll

Leader leader

Trace and Write.

Practice writing a lowercase l.

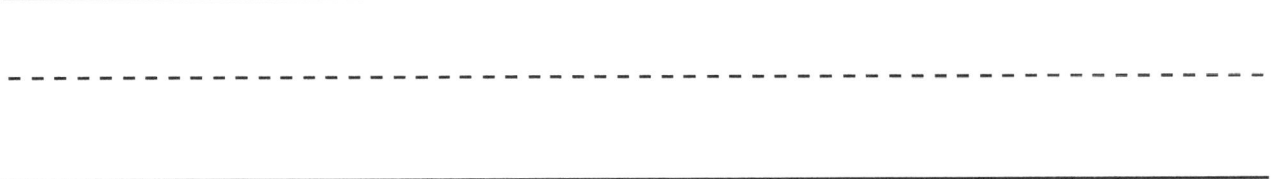

Trace and Write.

Practice writing an uppercase L.

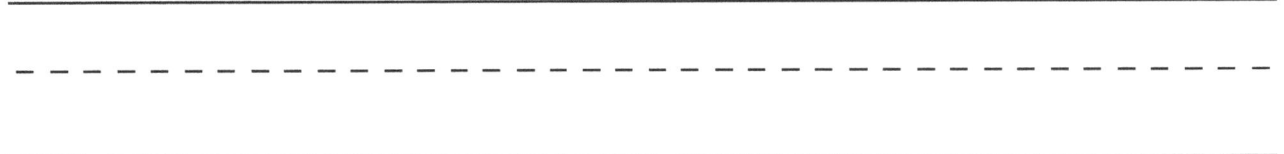

Trace.

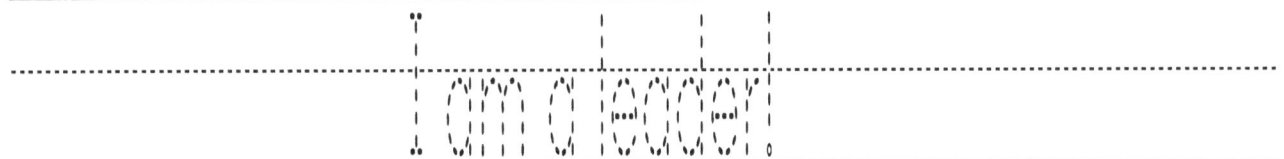

I am a leader.

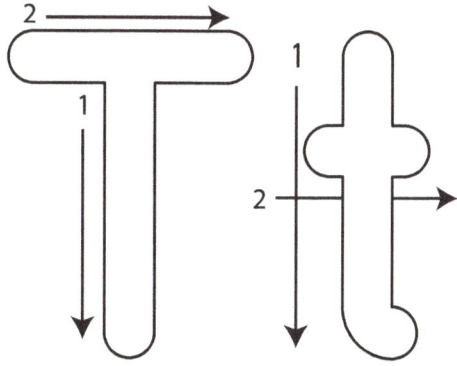

T t

turkey

Trace and write

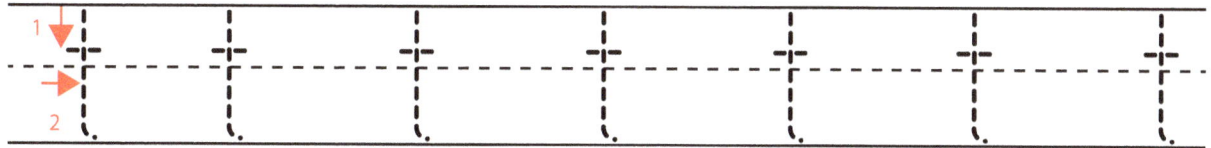

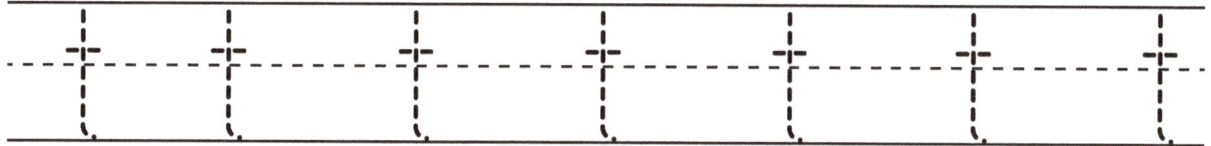

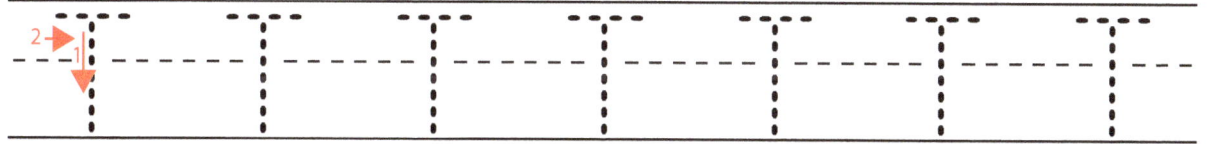

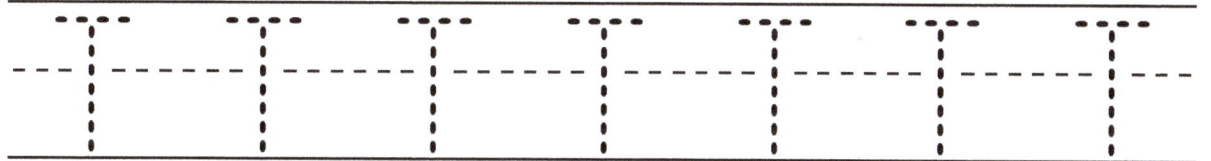

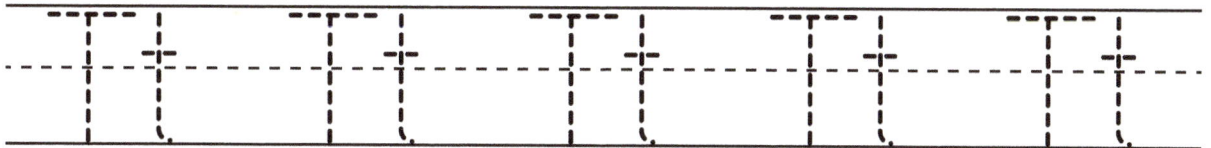

t t t t t t t t

t t t t t t t

T T T T T T

T T T T T T

Tt Tt Tt Tt Tt

Trustworthy trustworthy

Trace and Write.

t t

t

Practice writing a lowercase t.

Trace and Write.

T T

T

Practice writing an uppercase T.

Trace.

I am trustworthy!

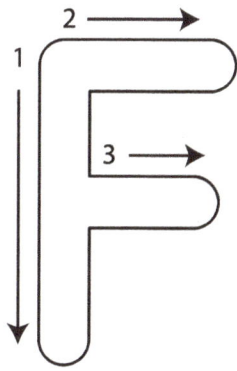

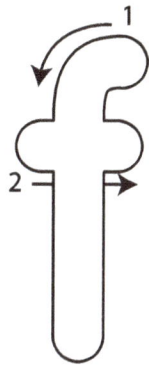

F f

fish

Trace and write

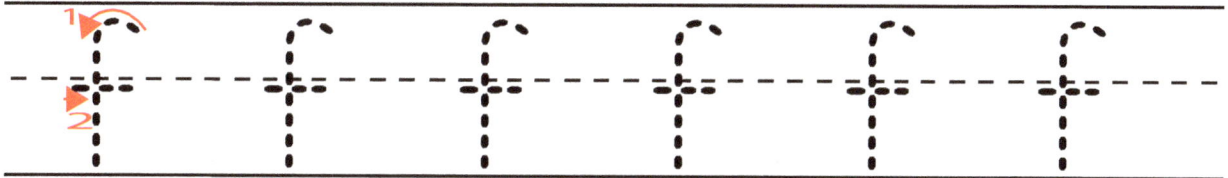

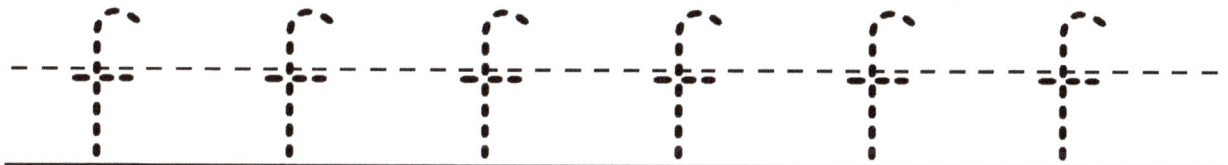

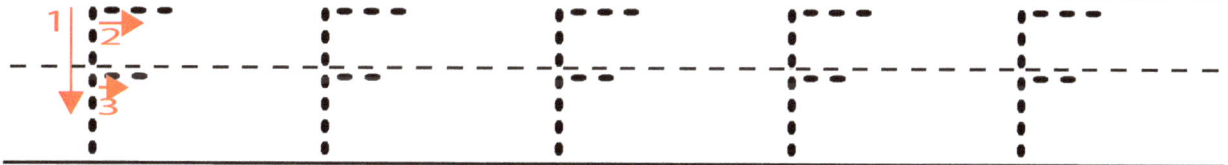

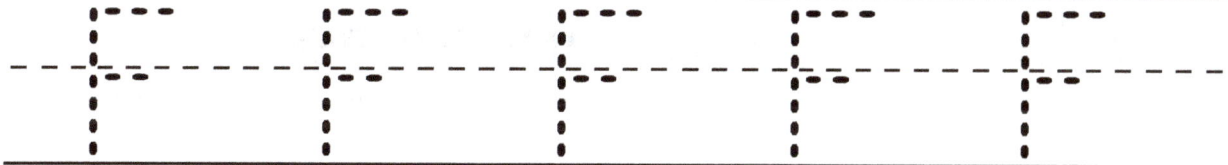

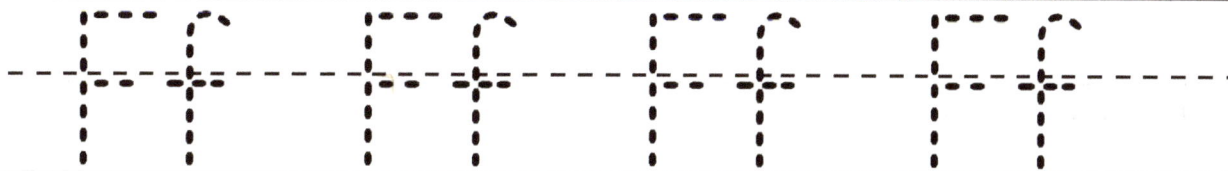

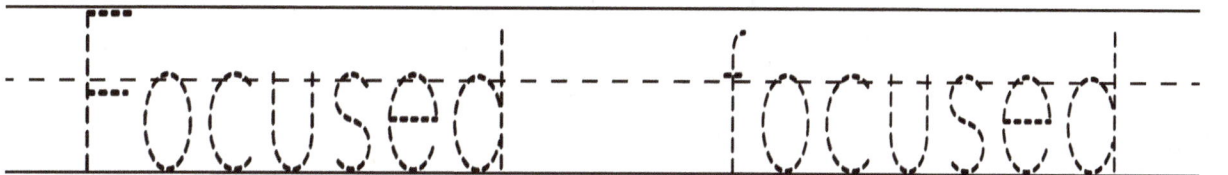

f f f f f f

f f f f f f

F F F F F F

F F F F F F

Ff Ff Ff Ff Ff

Focused focused

Trace and Write.

f   f

f

Practice writing a lowercase f.

Trace and Write.

F   F

F

Practice writing an uppercase F.

Trace.

I am focused.

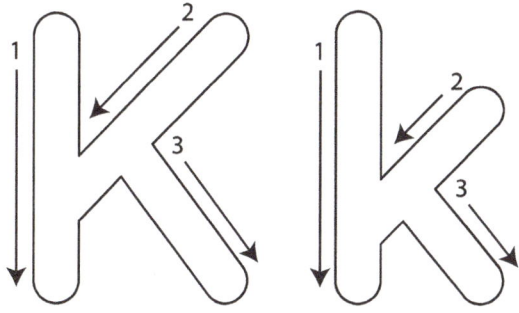

Kk

koala

Trace and write

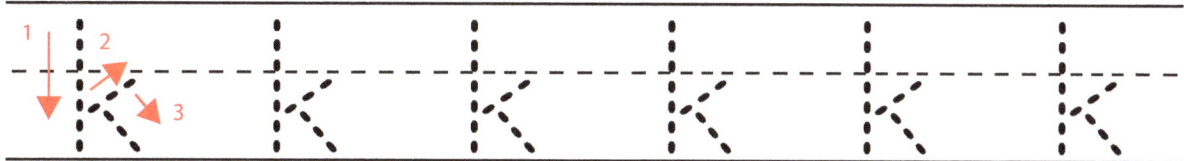

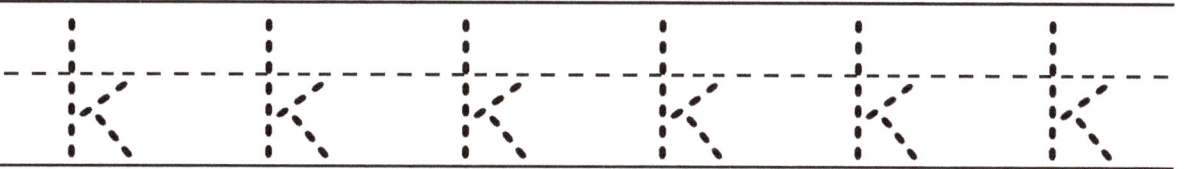

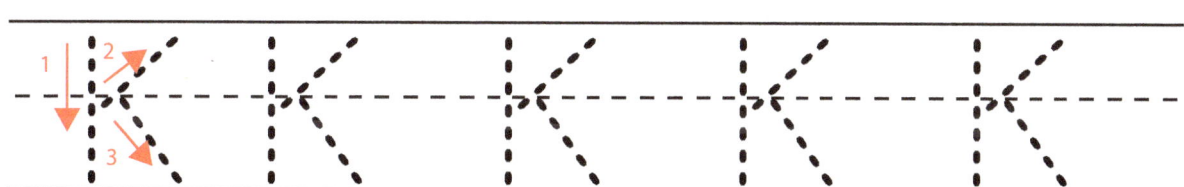

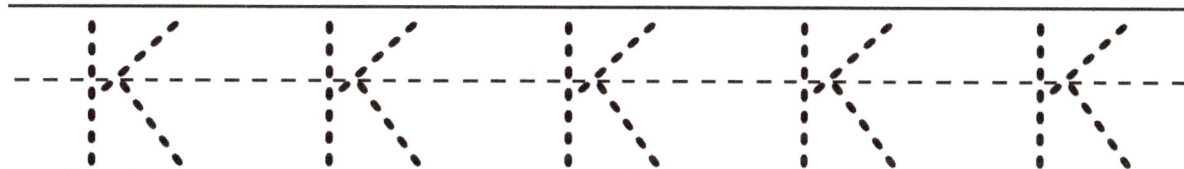

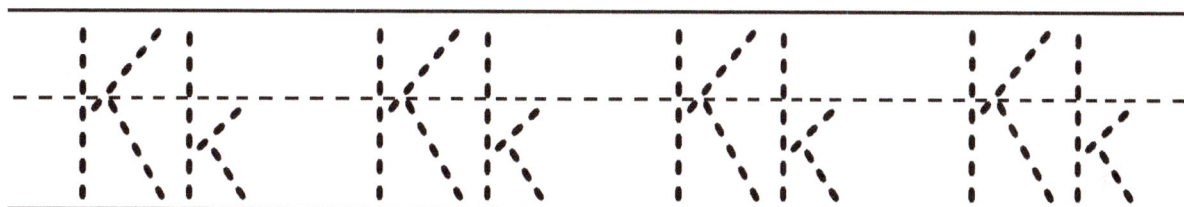

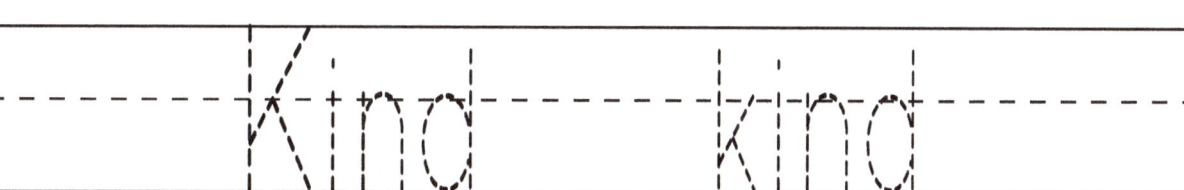

k k k k k k

k k k k k k

K K K K K

K K K K K

Kk Kk Kk Kk

Kind   kind

Trace and Write.

k k

k

Practice writing a lowercase k.

Trace and Write.

K K

K

Practice writing an uppercase K.

Trace.

I am kind!

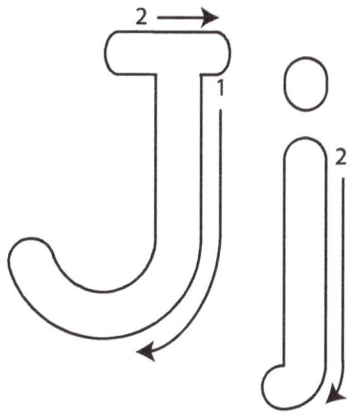

Jj

Trace and write

Trace and Write.

j j

j

Practice writing a lowercase j.

Trace and Write.

J J

J

Practice writing an uppercase J.

Trace.

I am joyful

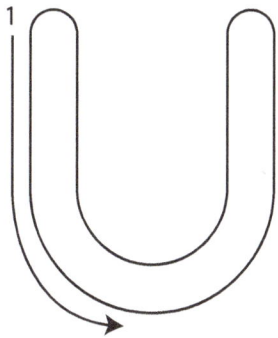

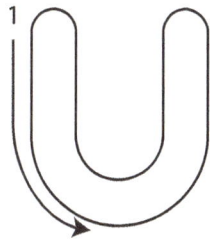

U u

unicorn

Trace and write

U u u u u u u

u u u u u u u

U U U U U U

U U U U U U

Uu Uu Uu

Unique   unique

Trace and Write.

U   U

U

Practice writing a lowercase r.

Trace and Write.

U   U

U

Practice writing an uppercase U.

Trace.

I am unique

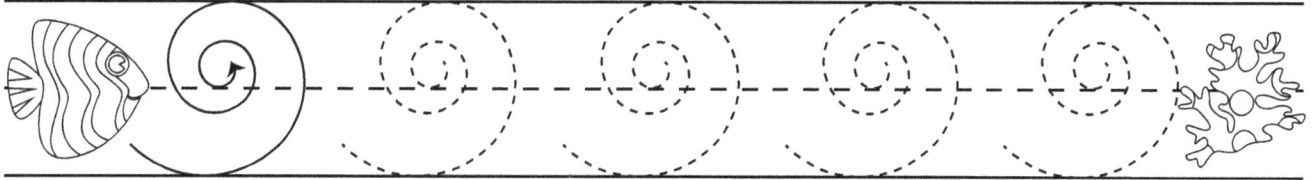

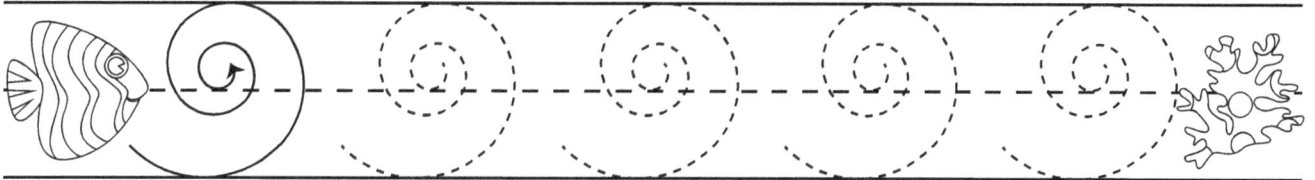

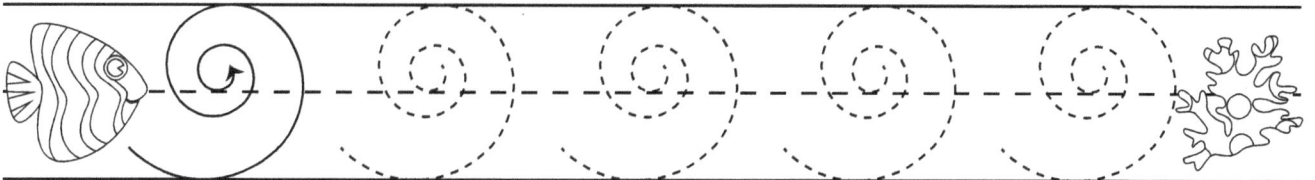

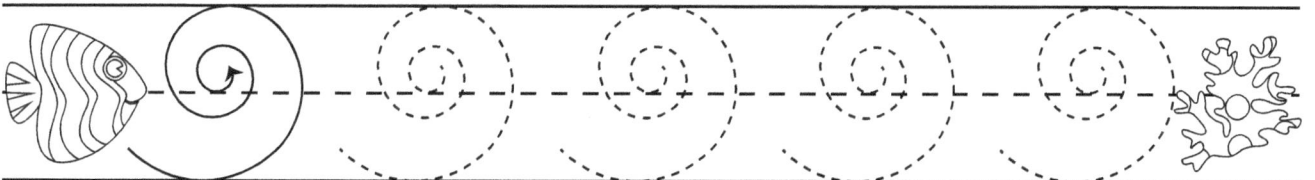

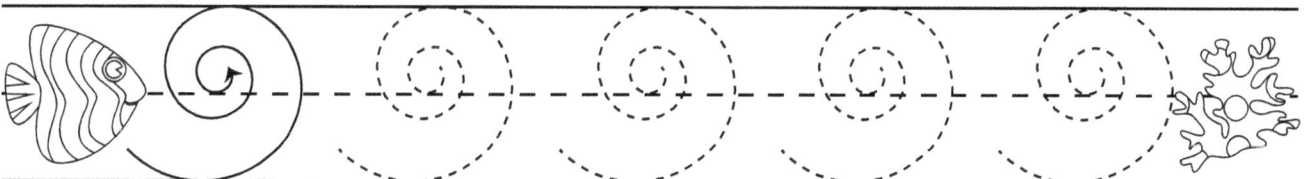

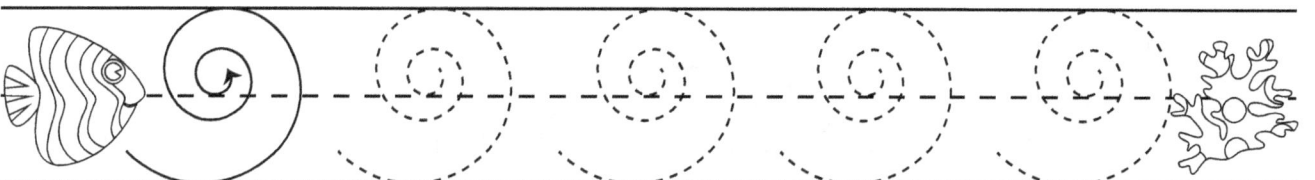

Cc

cab

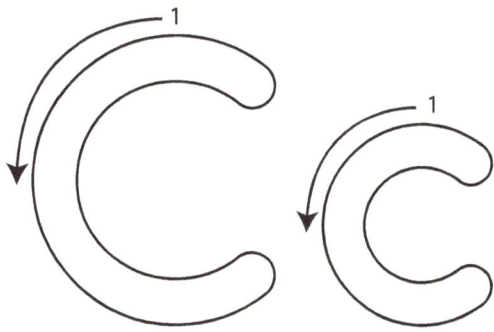

Trace and write

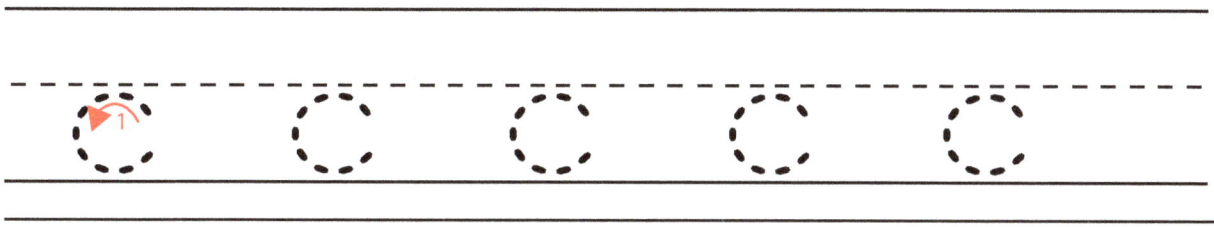

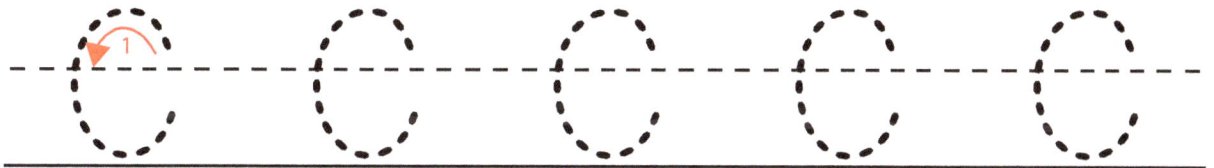

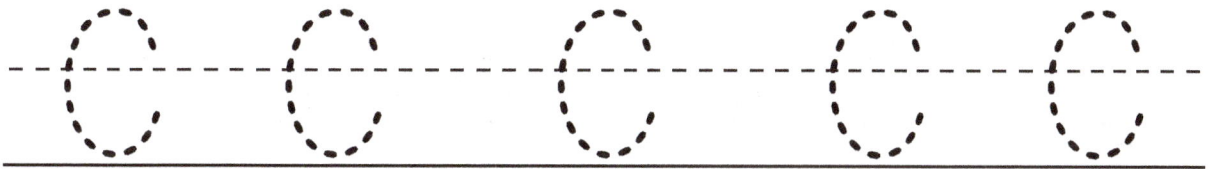

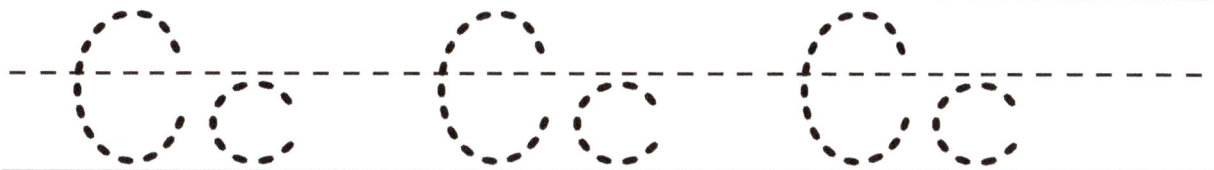

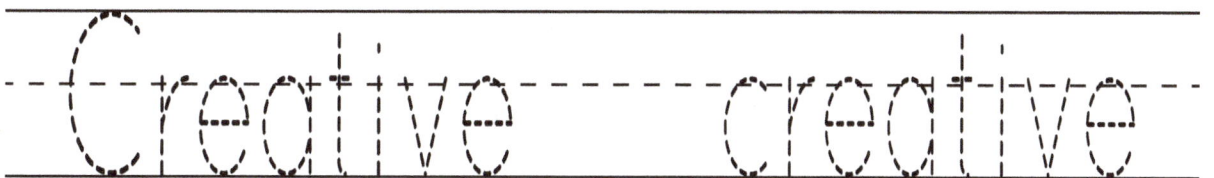

c c c c c

c c c c c

C C C C C

C C C C C

Cc Cc Cc

Creative   creative

Trace and Write.

C   C

C

Practice writing a lowercase c.

Trace and Write.

C   C

C

Practice writing an uppercase C.

Trace.

I am creative!

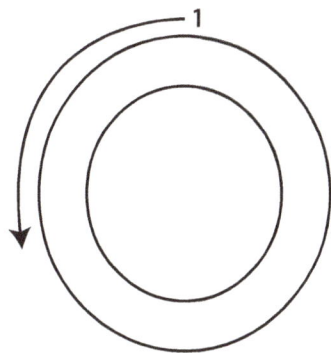

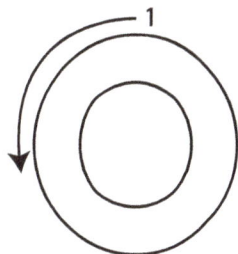

octopus

Trace and write

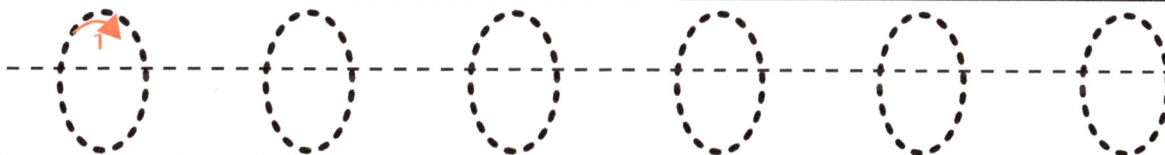

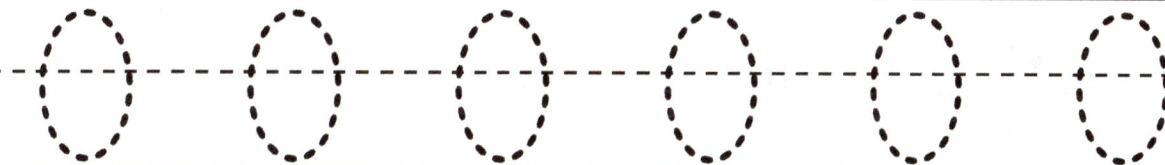

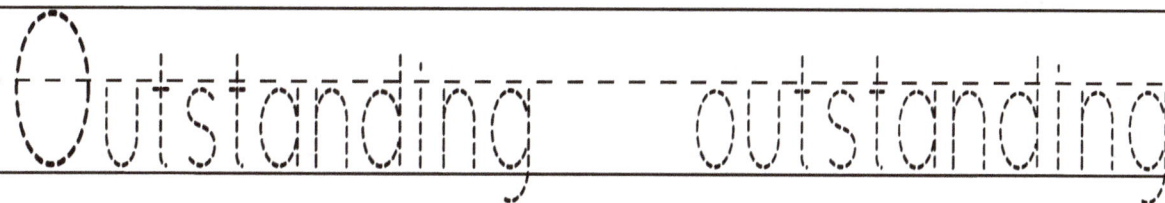

O o o o o o o o

O o o o o o

O o o o o o

O o o o o o

Oo Oo Oo Oo

Outstanding outstanding

Trace and Write.

O O

O

Practice writing a lowercase o.

Trace and Write.

O O

O

Practice writing an uppercase O.

Trace.

I am outstanding!

A a

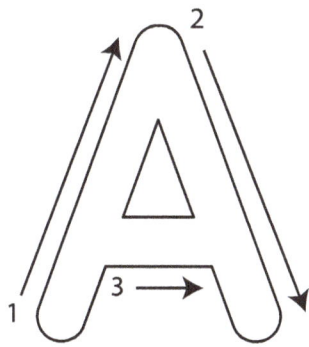

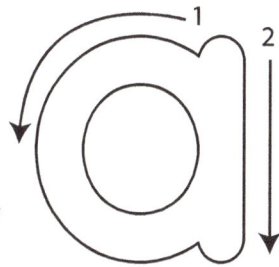

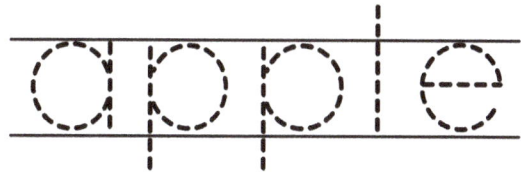

Trace and write

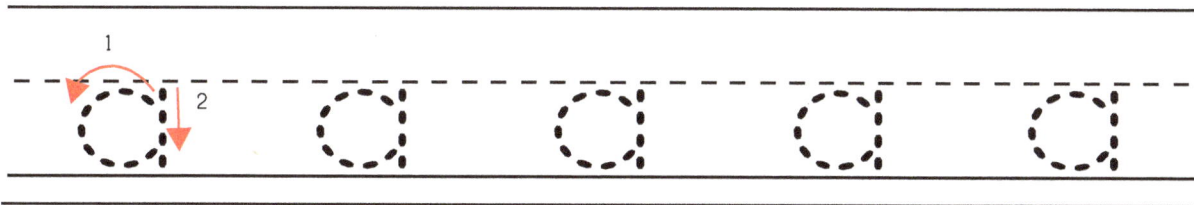

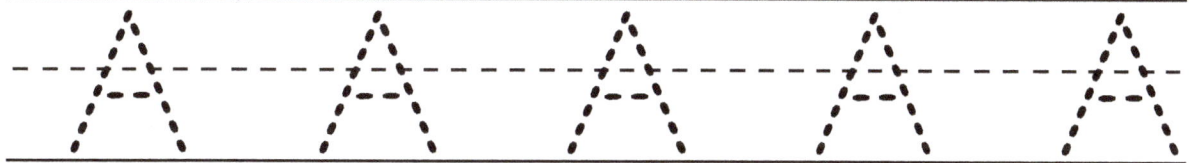

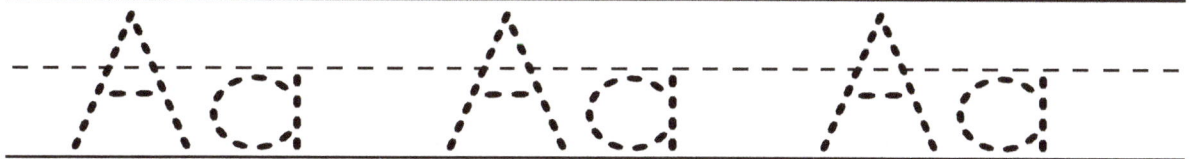

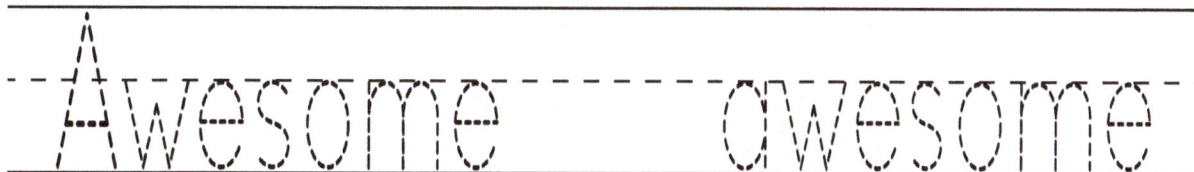

apple

a a a a a

a a a a a

A A A A A

A A A A A

Aa Aa Aa

Awesome awesome

Trace and Write.

a a

a

Practice writing a lowercase a.

Trace and Write.

A A

A

Practice writing an uppercase A.

Trace.

I am awesome!

D d

desk

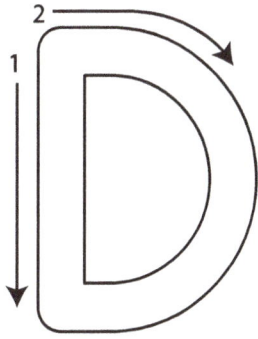

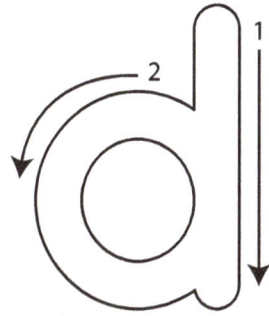

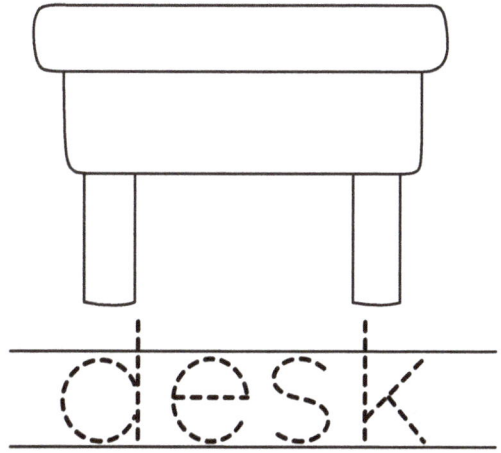

Trace and write

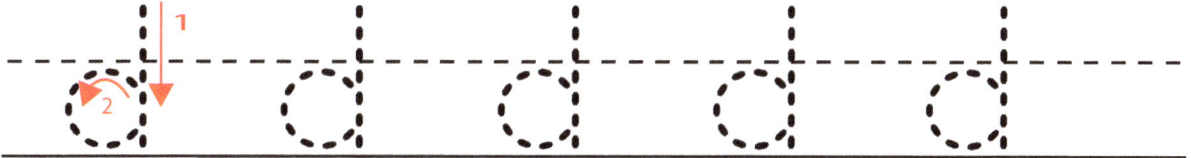

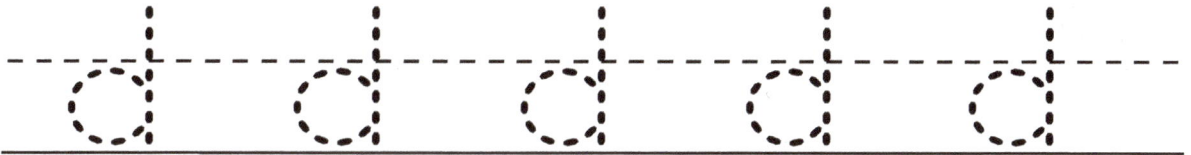

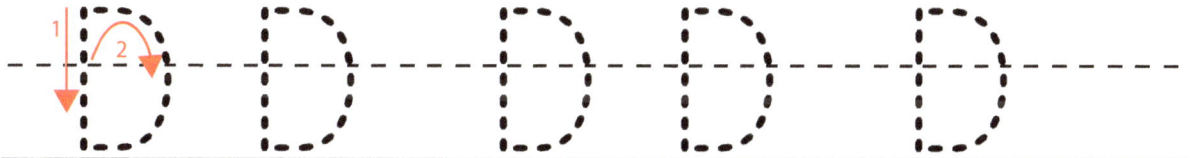

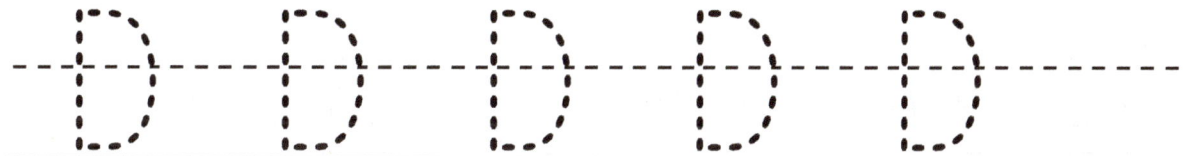

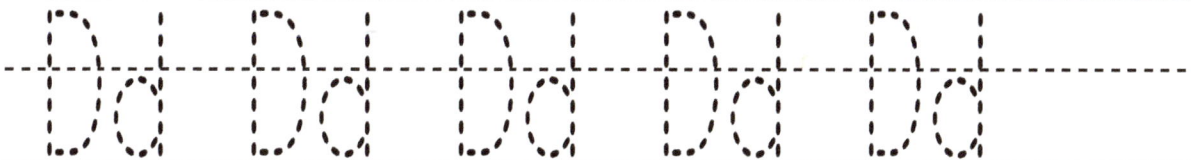

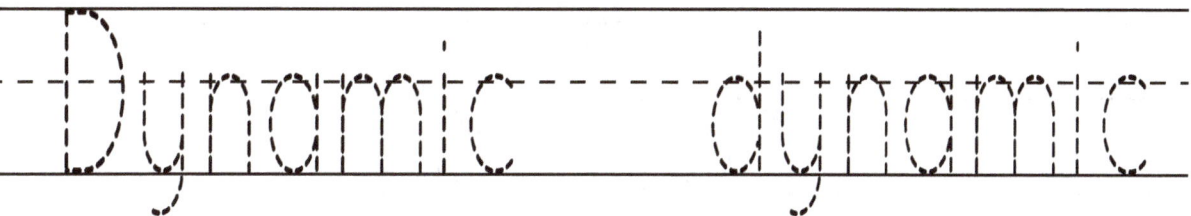

d d d d d

d d d d d

D D D D D

D D D D D

Dd Dd Dd Dd Dd

Dynamic dynamic

Trace and Write.

d　d

d

Practice writing a lowercase d.

Trace and Write.

D　D

D

Practice writing an uppercase D.

Trace.

I am dynamic!

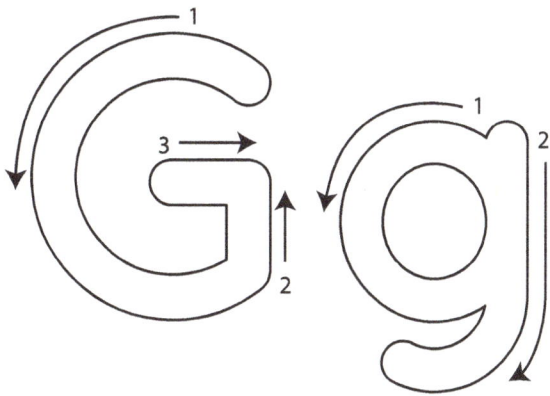

G g

goat

Trace and write

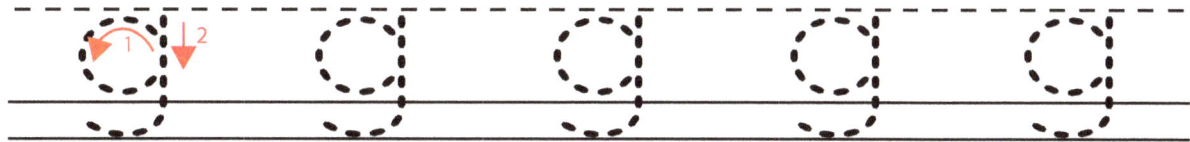

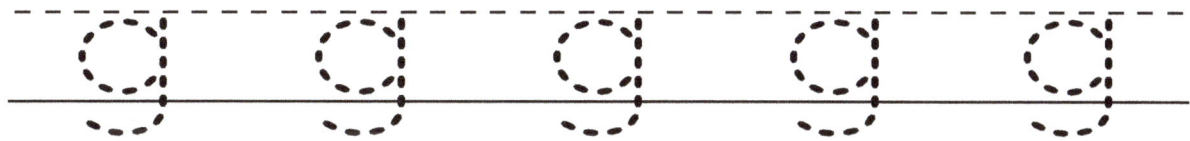

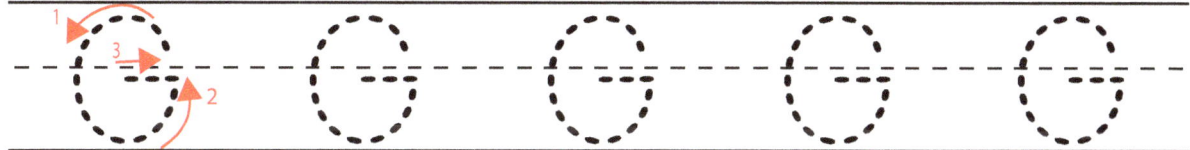

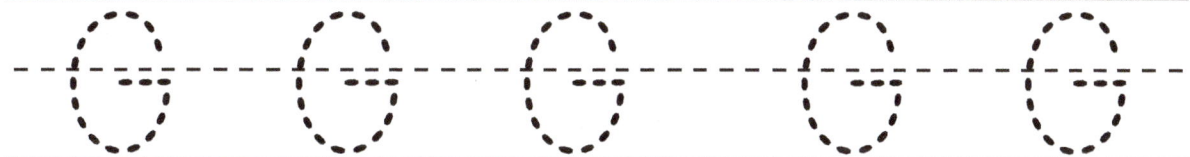

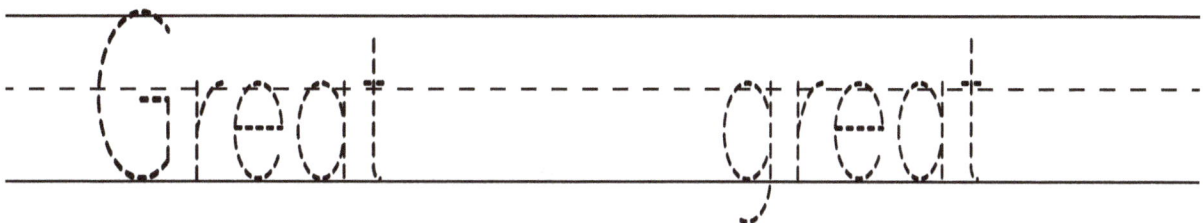

g g g g g

g g g g g

G G G G G

G G G G G

Gg Gg Gg

Great   great

Trace and Write.

g g

g

Practice writing a lowercase g.

Trace and Write.

G G

G

Practice writing an uppercase G.

Trace.

I am great!

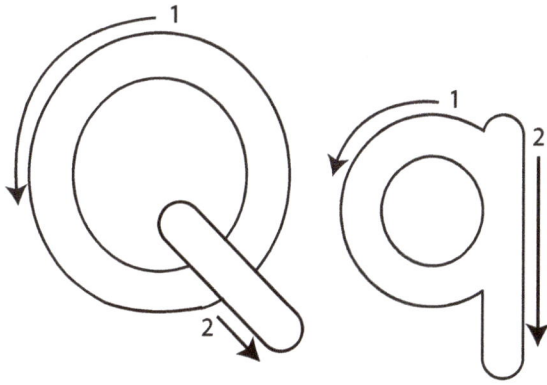

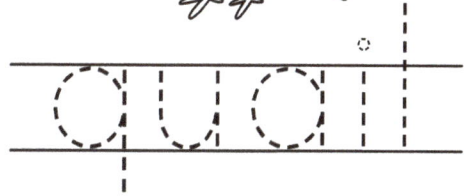

Trace and write

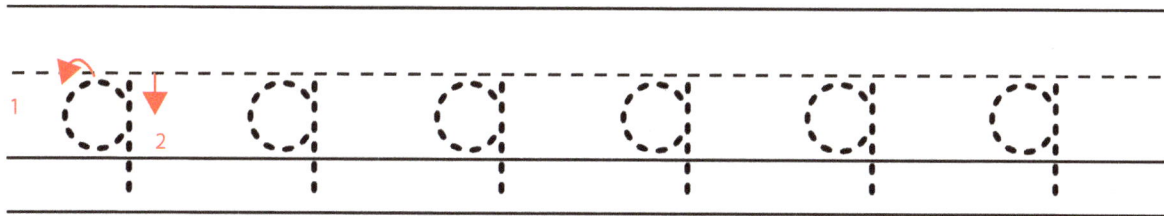

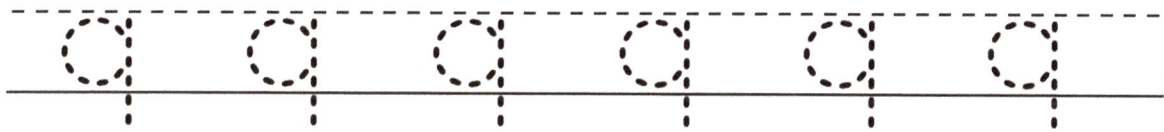

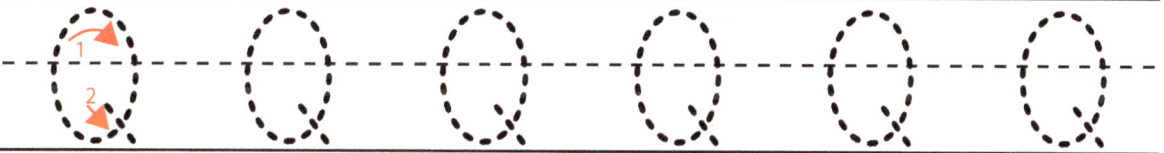

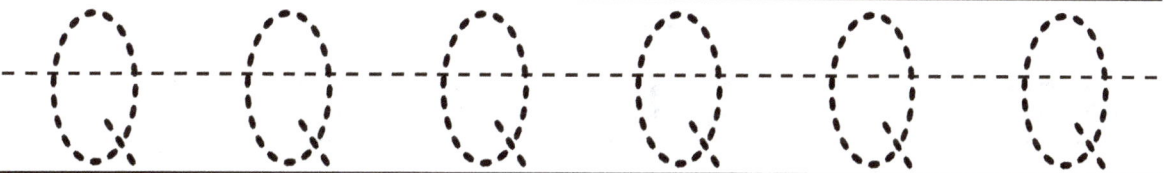

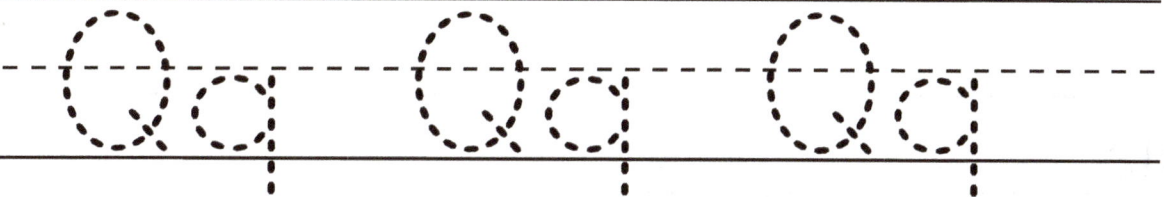

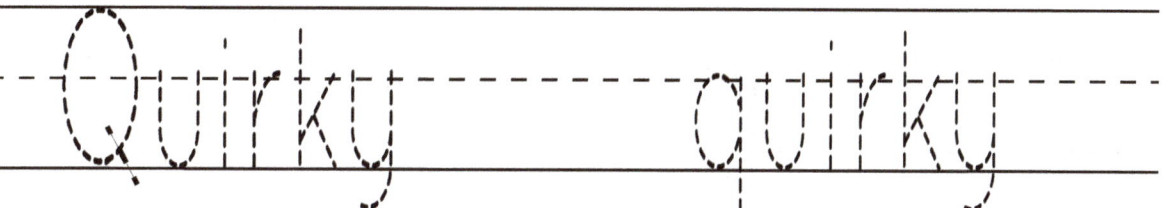

quail

Q q

q q q q q q

q q q q q q

O O O O O O

O O O O O O

Qq Qq Qq

Quirky   quirky

Trace and Write.

q   q

q

Practice writing a lowercase q.

Trace and Write.

Q   Q

Q

Practice writing an uppercase Q.

Trace.

I am quirky!

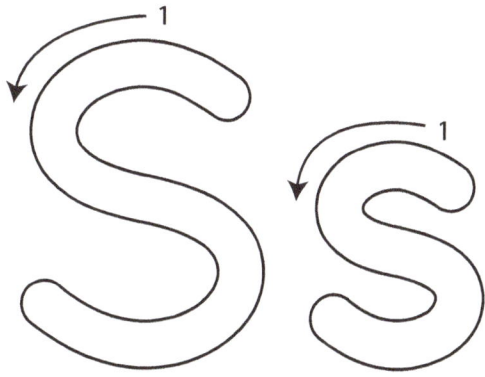

S s

sun

Trace and write

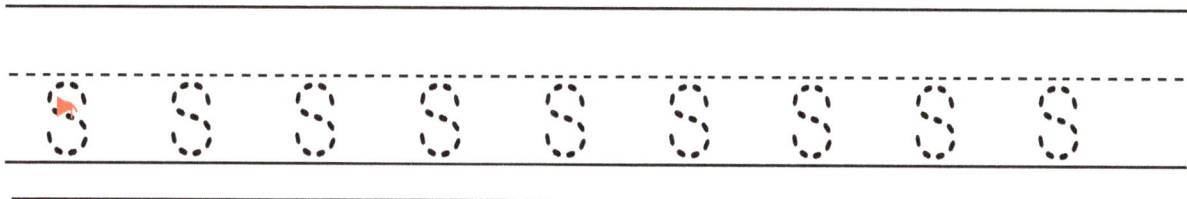

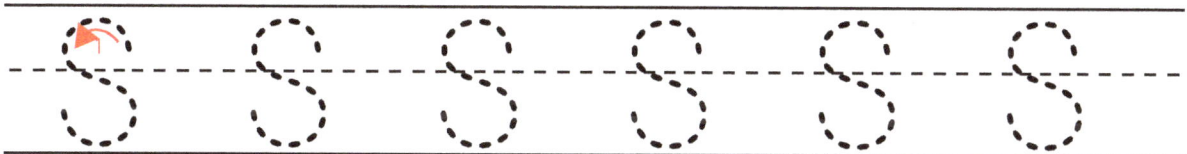

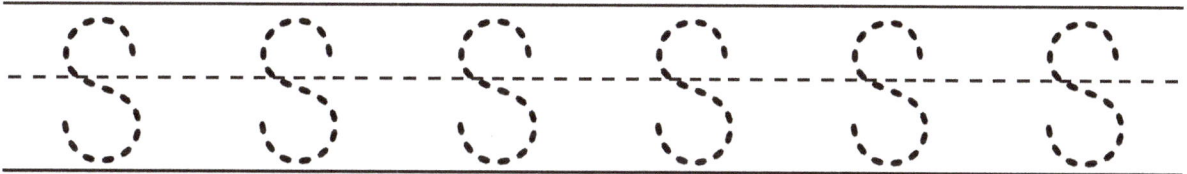

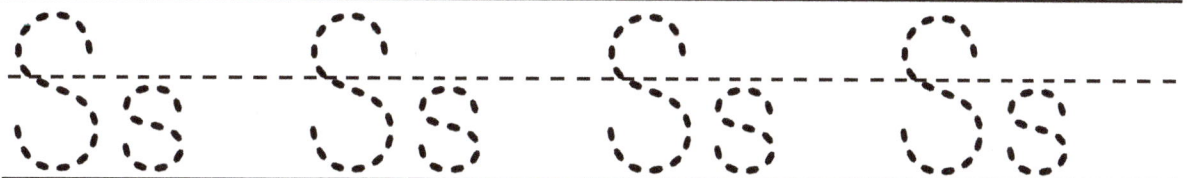

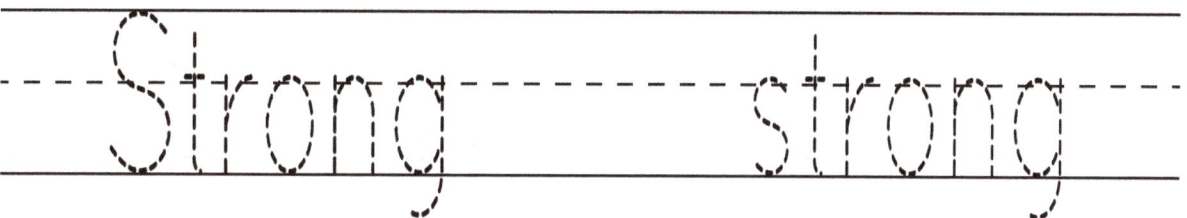

S S S S S S S S S

S S S S S S S

S S S S S S

S S S S S S

Ss Ss Ss Ss

Strong   strong

Trace and Write.

s   s

s

Practice writing a lowercase s.

Trace and Write.

S   S

S

Practice writing an uppercase S.

Trace and Write.

I am strong!

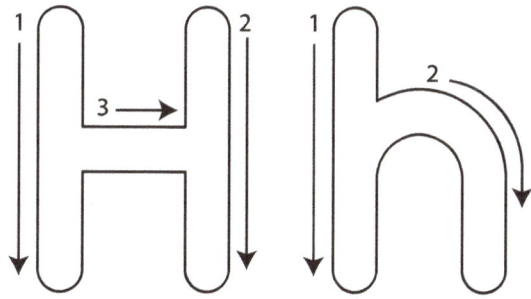

H h

hen

Trace and write

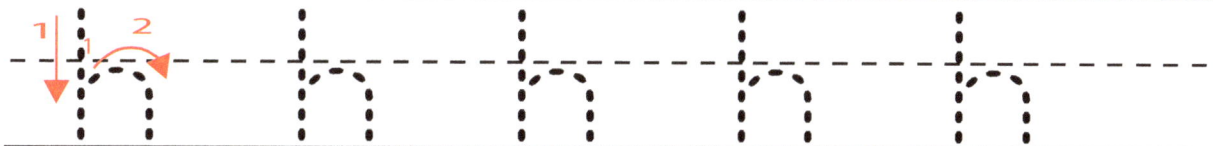

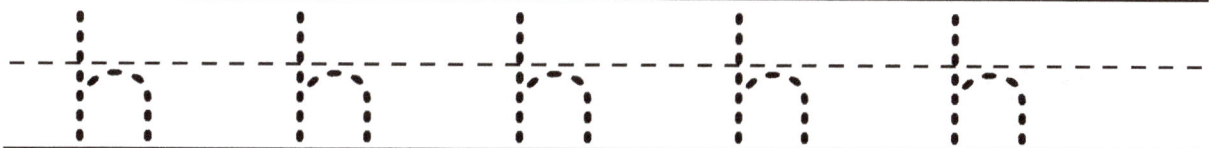

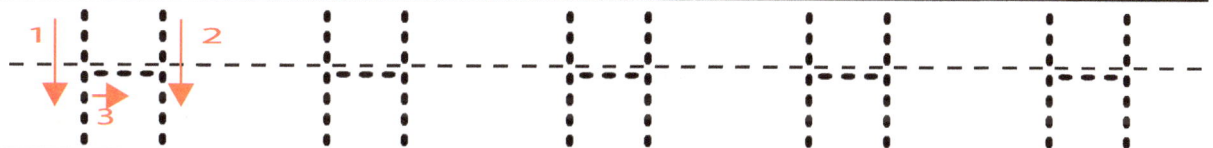

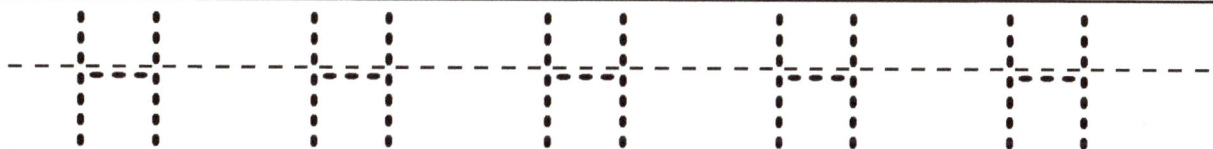

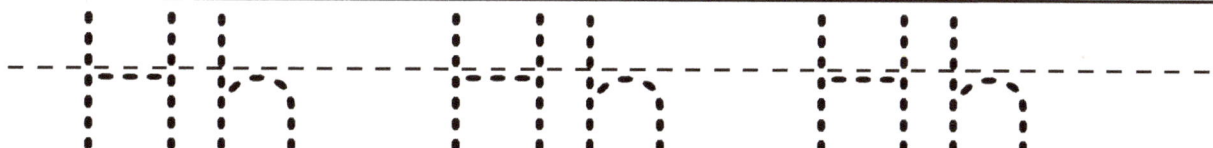

h   h   h   h   h

h   h   h   h   h

H   H   H   H   H

H   H   H   H   H

Hh   Hh   Hh

Helpful   helpful

Trace and Write.

h   h

h

Practice writing a lowercase h.

Trace and Write.

H   H

H

Practice writing an uppercase H.

Trace.

I am helpful!

B b

bee

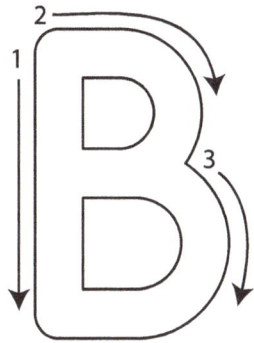

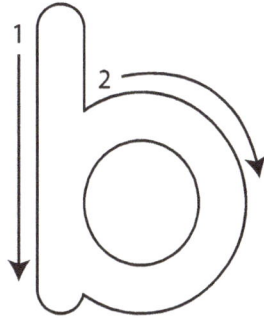

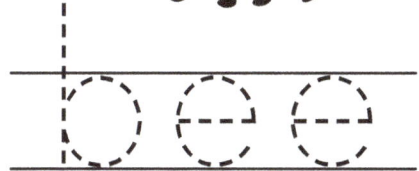

Trace and write

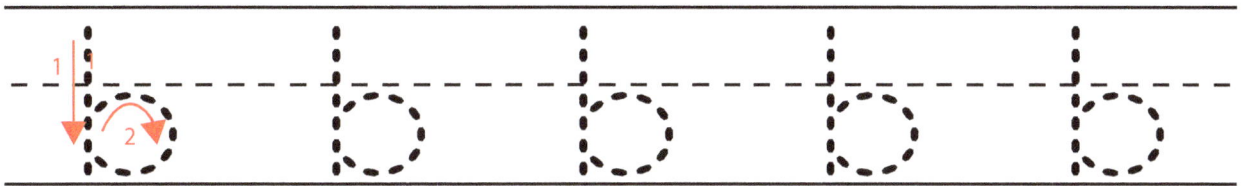

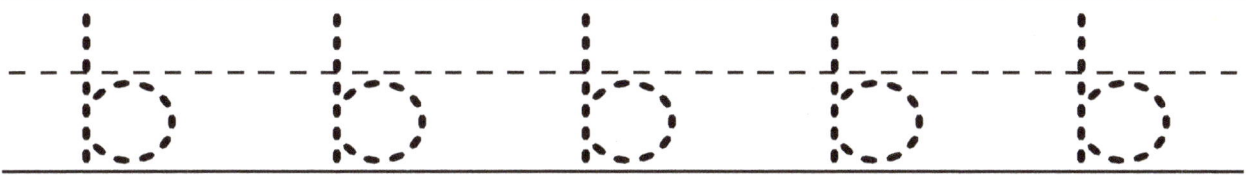

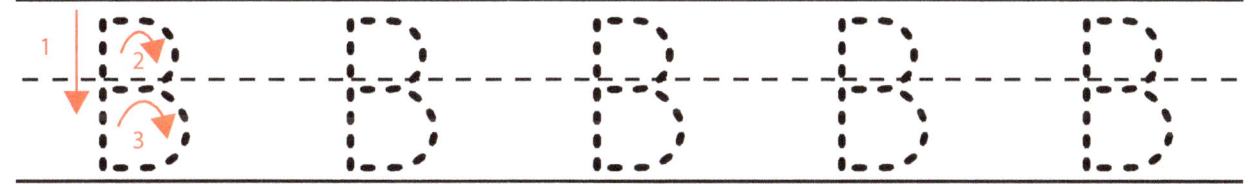

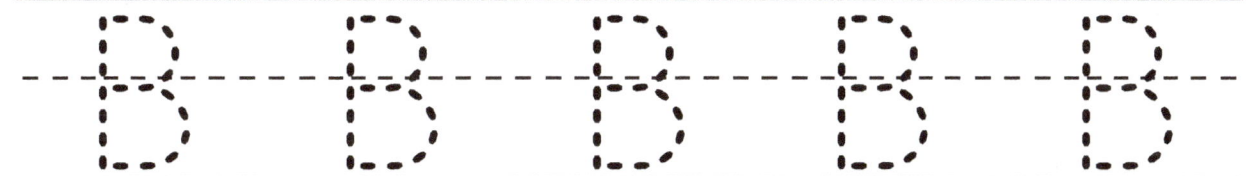

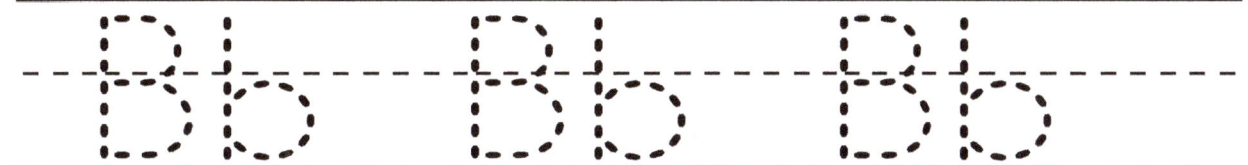

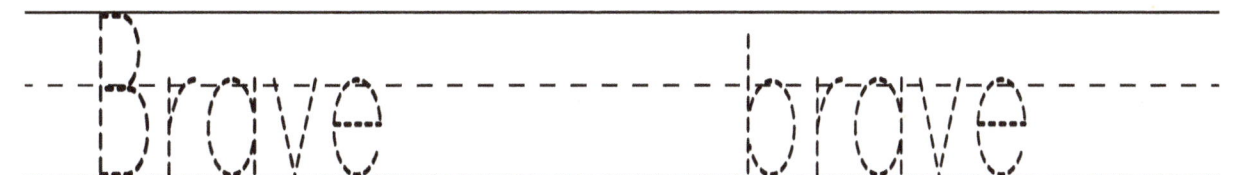

b b b b b

b b b b b

B B B B B

B B B B B

Bb Bb Bb

Brave brave

Trace and Write.

b　b

b

Practice writing a lowercase b.

Trace and Write.

B　B

B

Practice writing an uppercase B.

Trace.

I am brave!

P p

pear

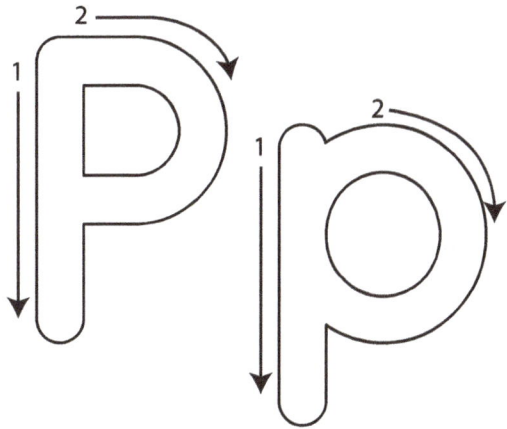

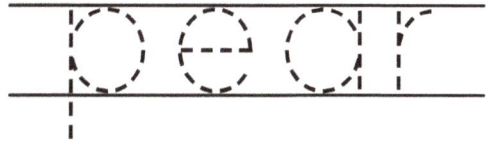

Trace and write

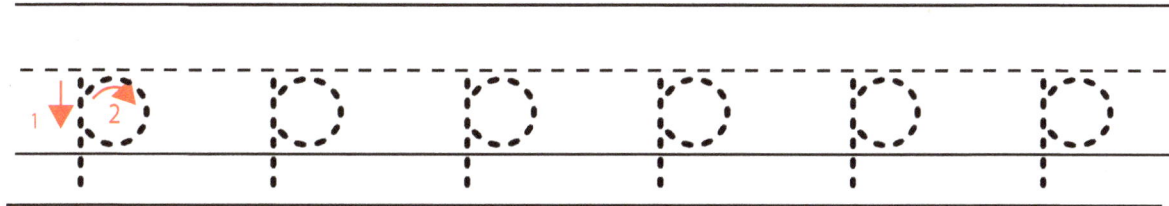

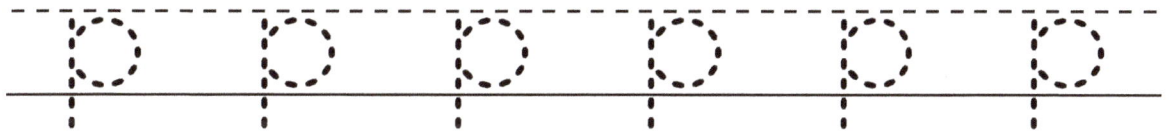

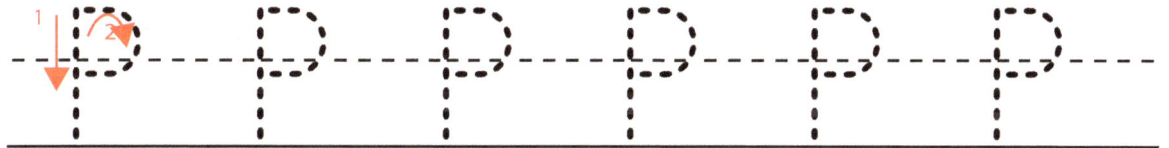

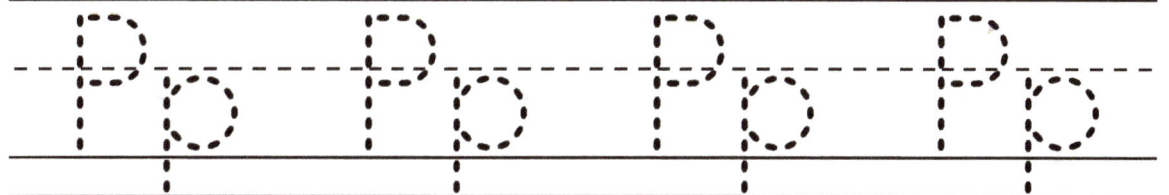

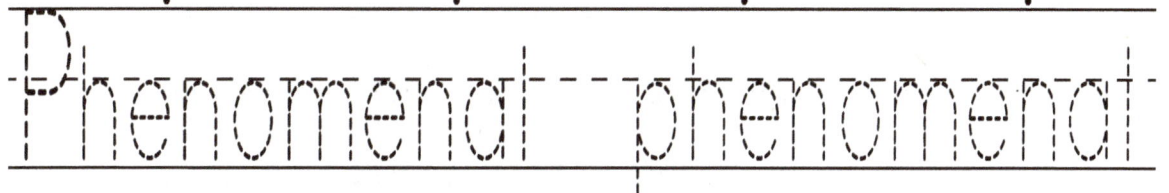

p p p p p p

p p p p p p

P P P P P P

P P P P P P

Pp Pp Pp Pp Pp

Phenomenal   phenomenal

Trace and Write.

p   p

p

Practice writing a lowercase p.

Trace and Write.

P   P

P

Practice writing an uppercase P.

Trace.

I am phenomenal!

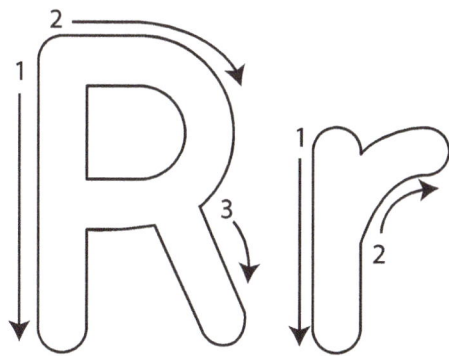

Rr

rocket

Trace and write

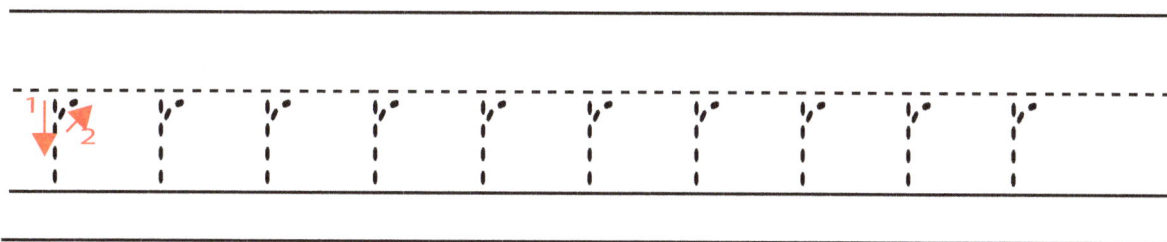

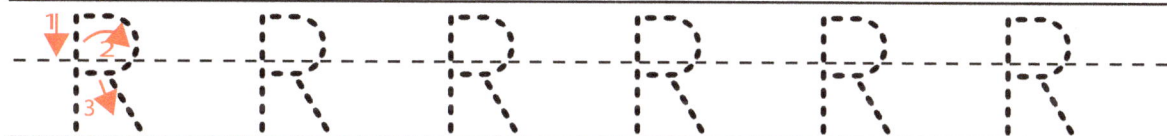

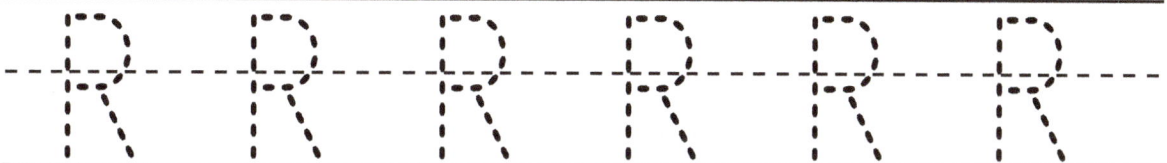

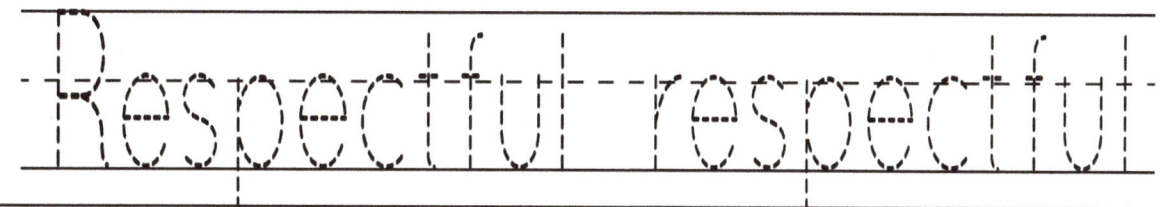

r r r r r r r r r

r r r r r r r r r

R R R R R R

R R R R R R

Rr Rr Rr Rr Rr

Respectful respectful

Trace and Write.

r   r

r

Practice writing a lowercase r.

Trace and Write.

R   R

R

Practice writing an uppercase R.

Trace.

I am respectful.

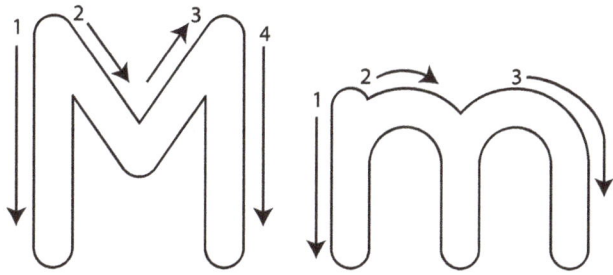

Mm

monkey

Trace and write

m m m m m

m m m m m

M M M M M

M M M M M

Mm Mm Mm

Marvelous marvelous

Trace and Write.

m

m   m

Practice writing a lowercase I.

Trace and Write.

M   M

M

Practice writing an uppercase M.

Trace.

I am marvelous!

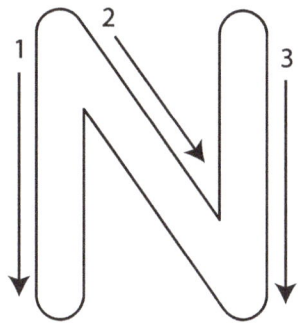

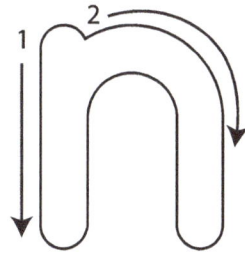

Nn

nurse

Trace and write

n n n n n n n n

n n n n n n n n

N N N N N N N N

N N N N N N N N

Nn Nn Nn Nn

Nice   nice

Trace and Write.

n n

n

Practice writing a lowercase n.

Trace and Write.

N N

N

Practice writing an uppercase N.

Trace.

I am nice.

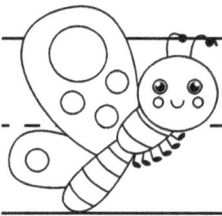

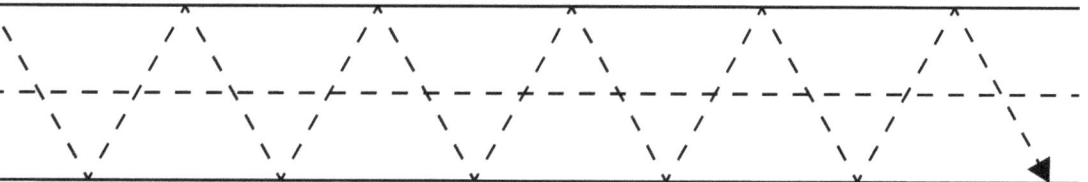

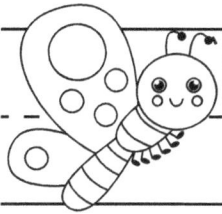

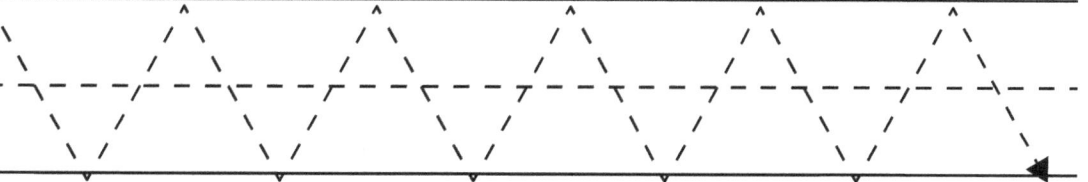

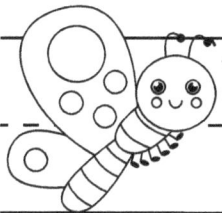

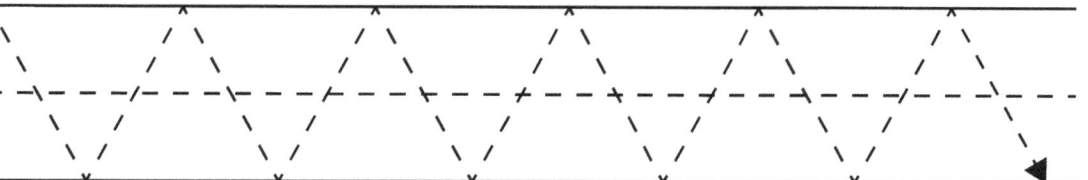

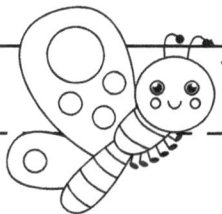

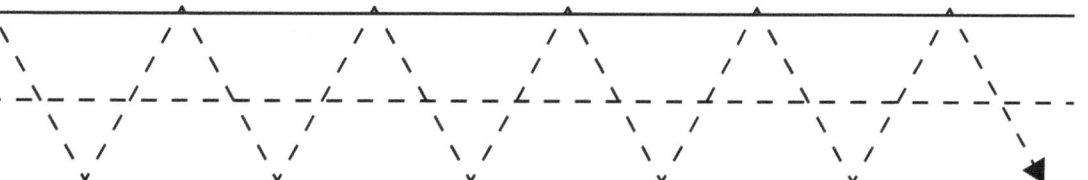

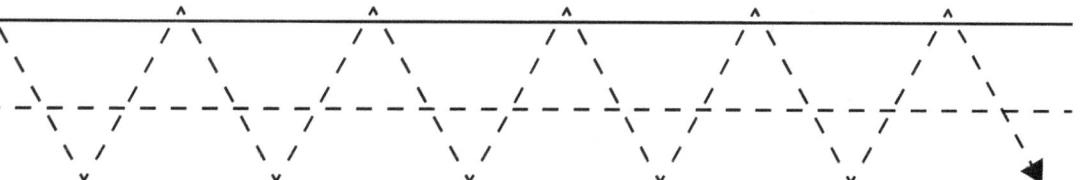

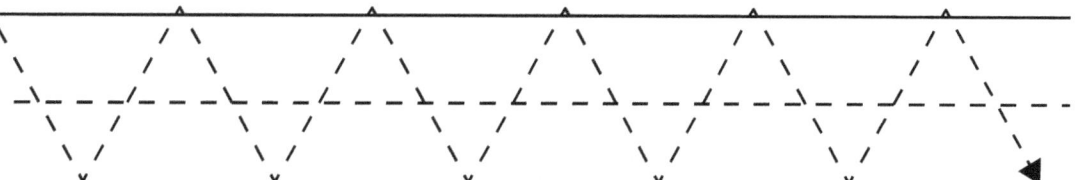

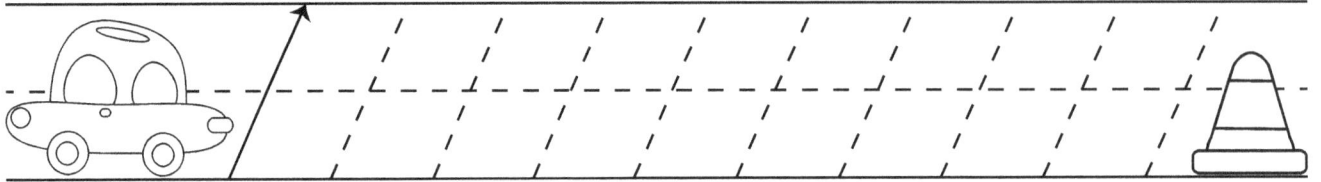

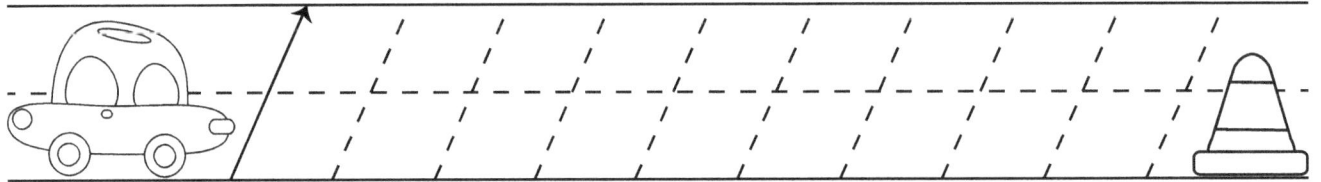

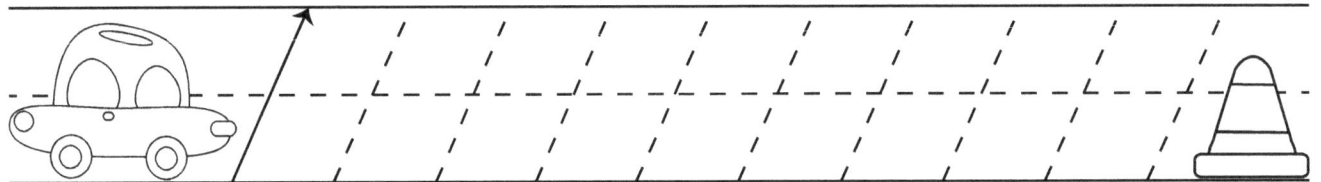

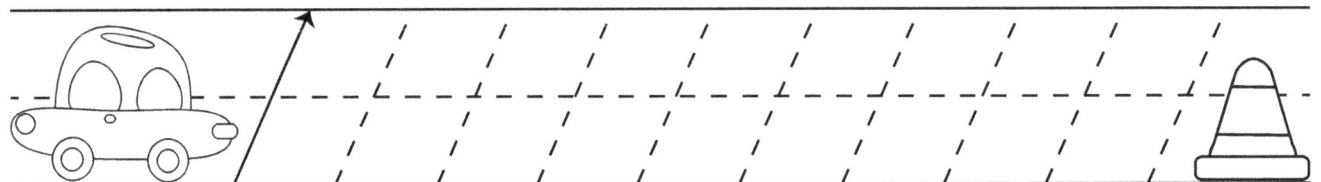

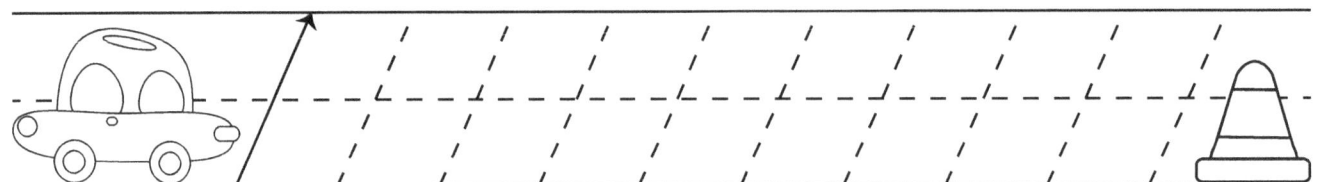

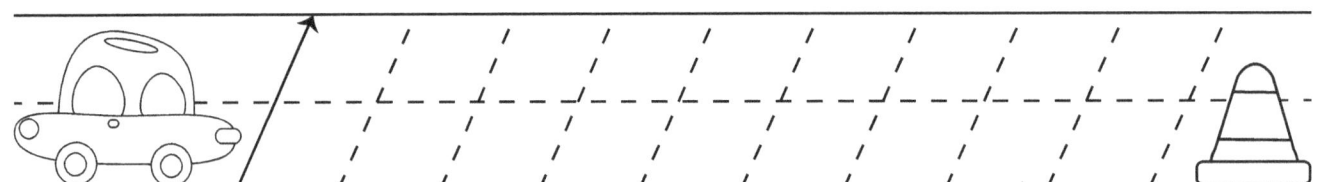

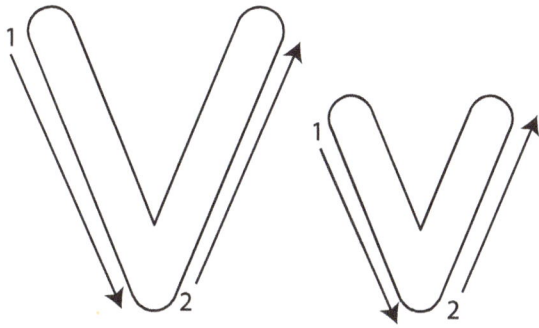

Trace and write

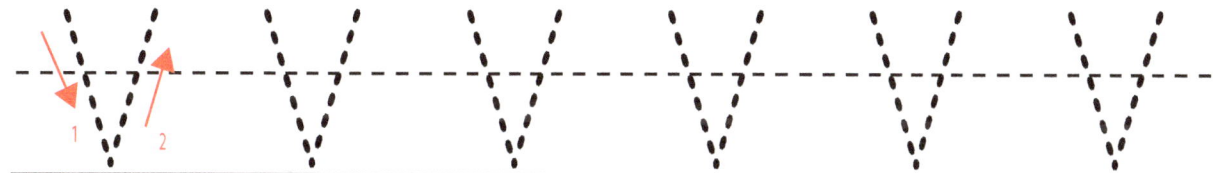

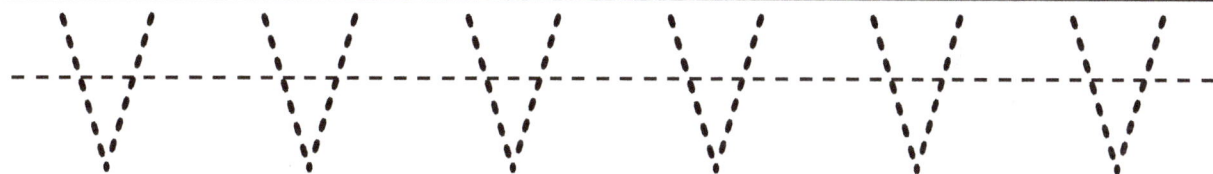

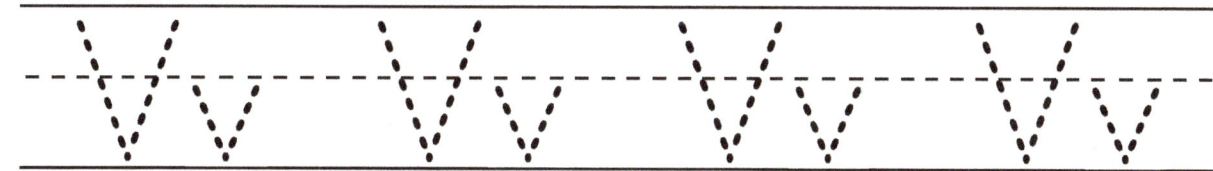

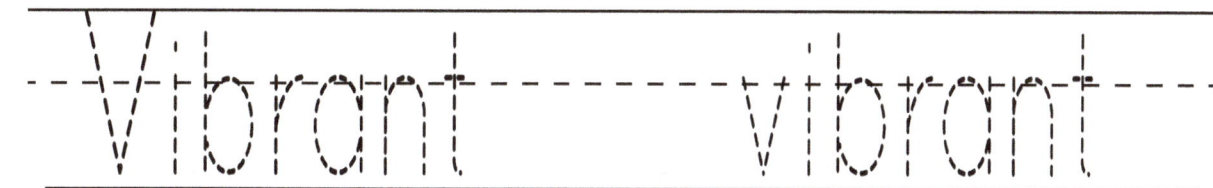

vulture

Vibrant   vibrant

Trace and Write.

v   v

v

Practice writing a lowercase v.

Trace and Write.

V   V

V

Practice writing an uppercase V.

Trace.

I am vibrant

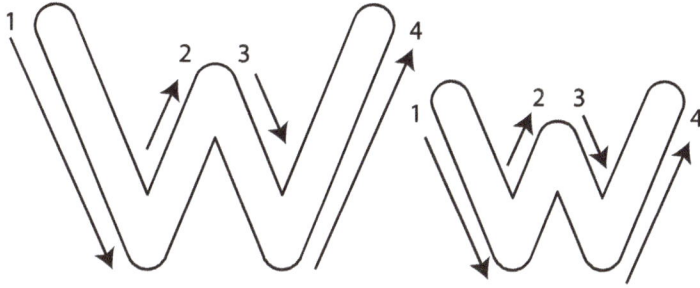

W w

whale

Trace and write

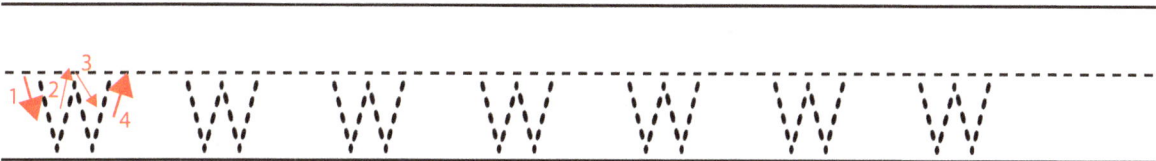

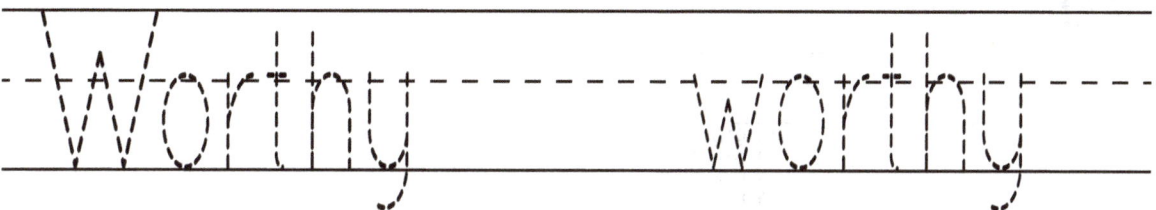

w w w w w w w

w w w w w w

W W W W W W

W W W W W W

Ww Ww Ww

Worthy   worthy

Trace and Write.

w w

w

Practice writing a lowercase w.

Trace and Write.

W W

W

Practice writing an uppercase W.

Trace.

I am worthy!

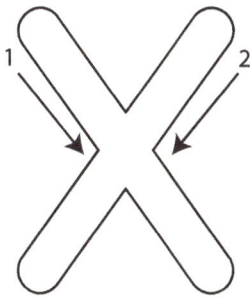

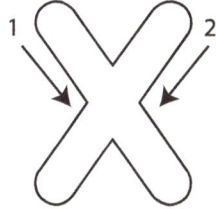

X x

x-ray fish

x-ray fish

Trace and write

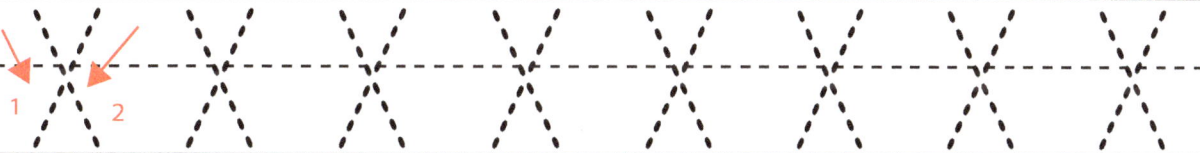

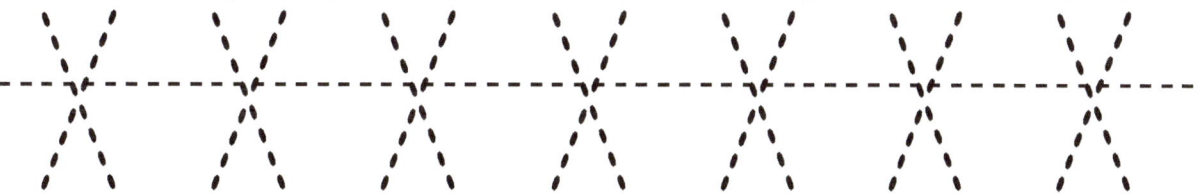

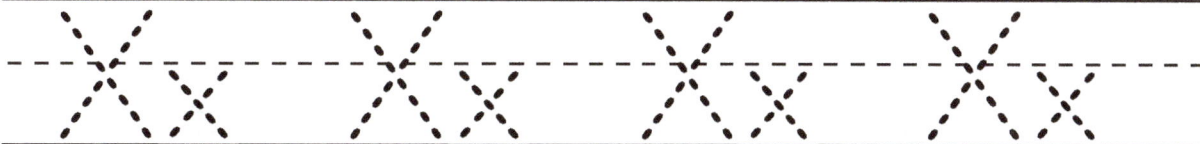

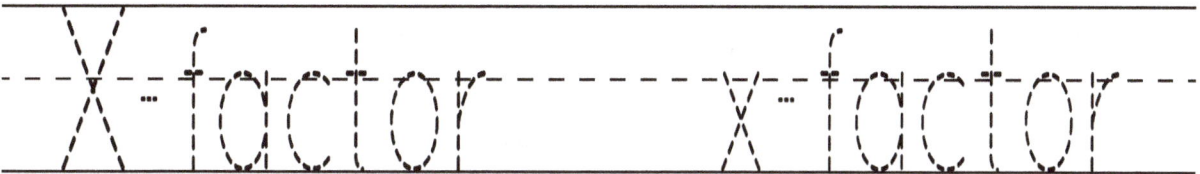

1 X 2   X   X   X   X   X   X

X   X   X   X   X   X   X

1 X 2   X   X   X   X   X   X

X   X   X   X   X   X   X

Xx   Xx   Xx   Xx

X-factor   X-factor

Trace and Write.

X   X

X

Practice writing a lowercase x.

Trace and Write.

X   X

X

Practice writing an uppercase X.

Trace.

I am a X factor!

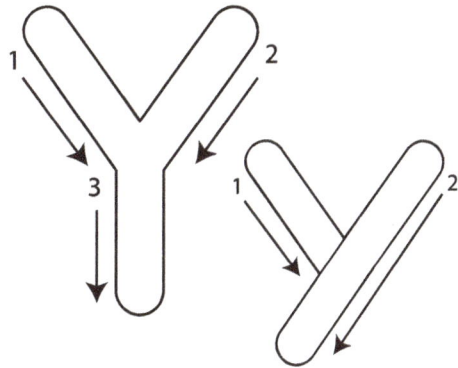

Y y

yak

Trace and write

Y Y Y Y Y Y Y Y Y

Y Y Y Y Y Y Y Y

Y Y Y Y Y Y Y

Y Y Y Y Y Y

Yy Yy Yy Yy

Youthful   youthful

Trace and Write.

Y Y

Y

Practice writing a lowercase y.

Trace and Write.

Y Y

Y

Practice writing an uppercase Y.

Trace.

I am youthful!

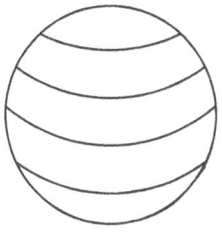

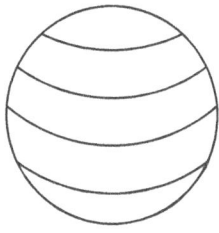

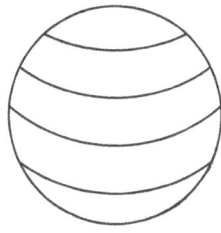

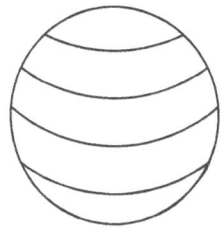

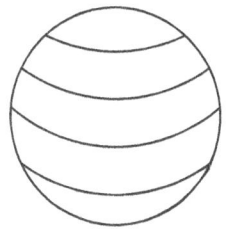

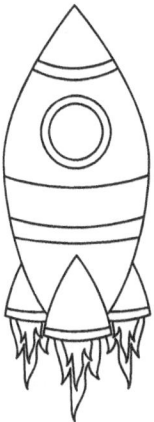

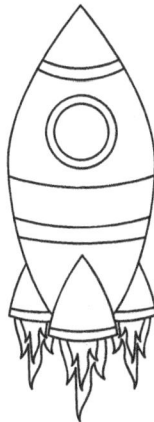

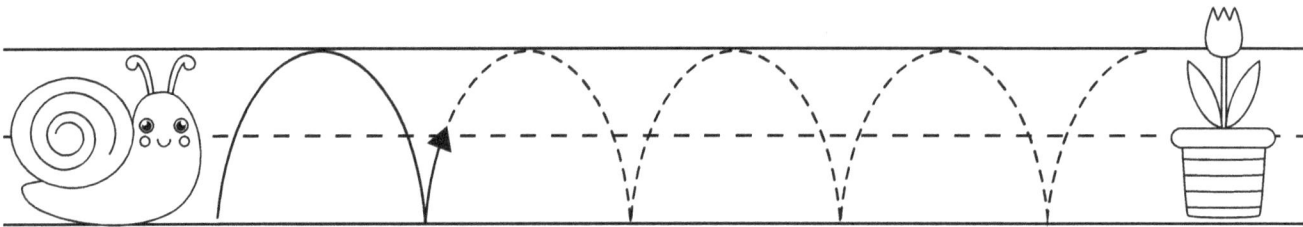

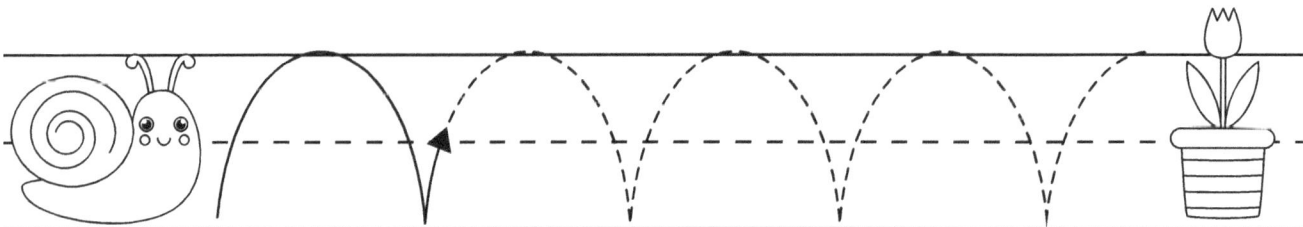

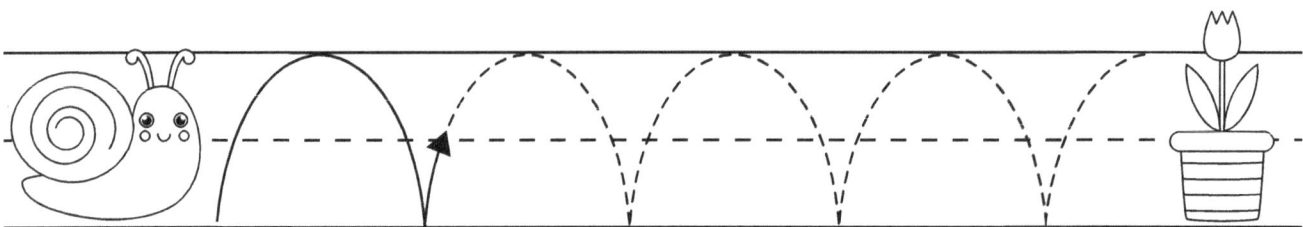

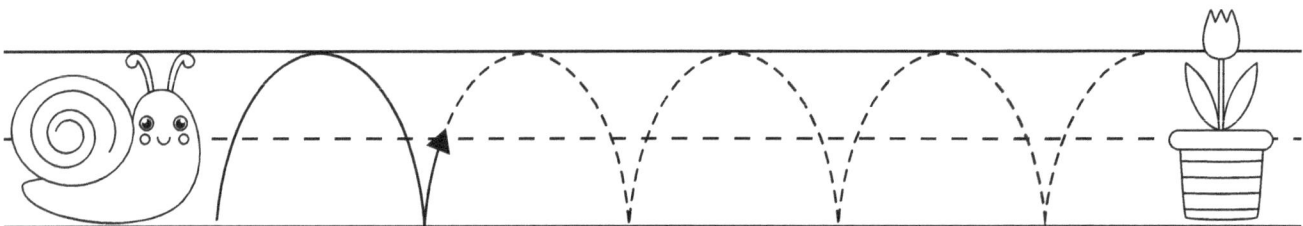

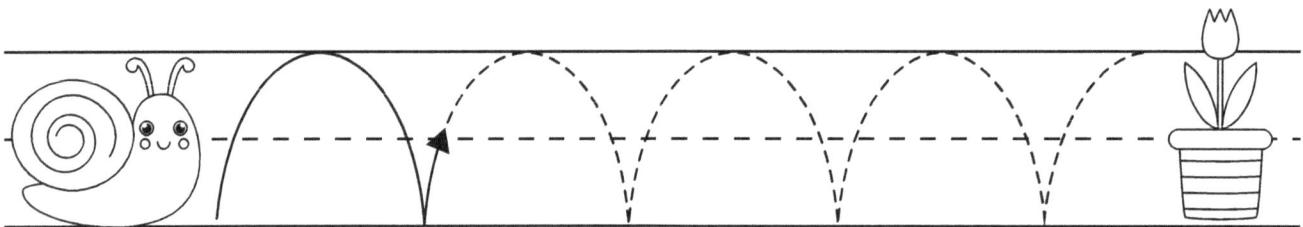

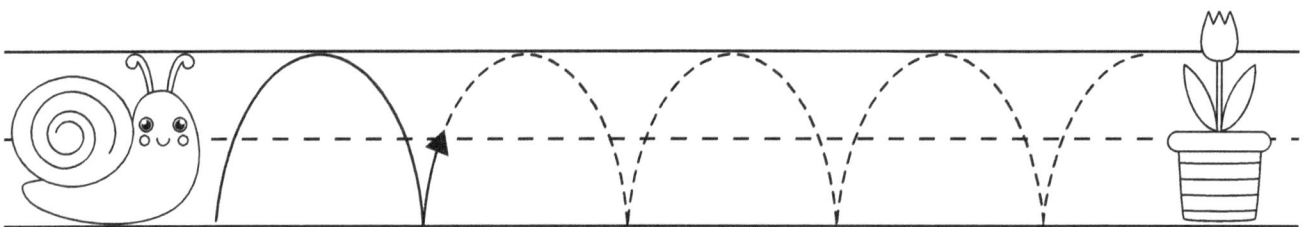

E e

egg

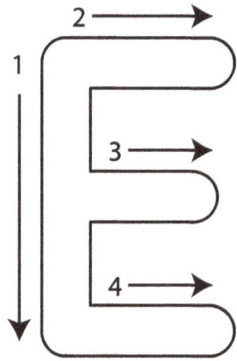

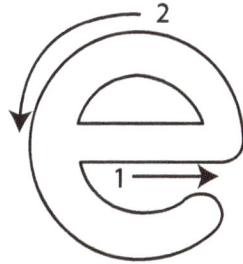

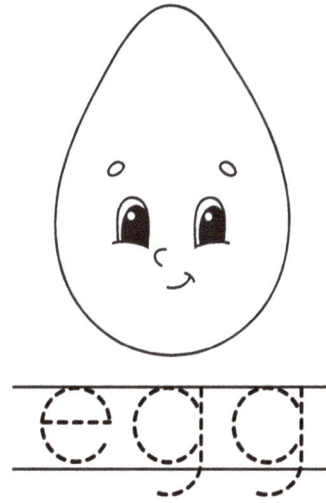

Trace and write

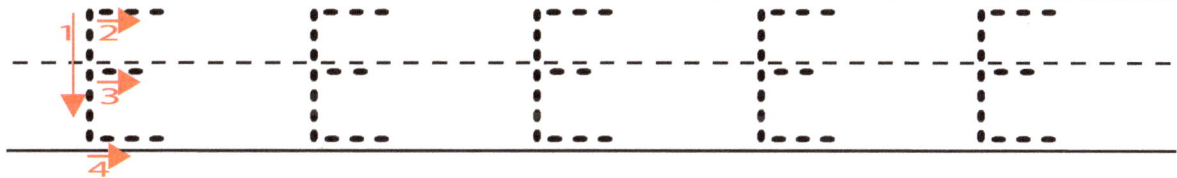

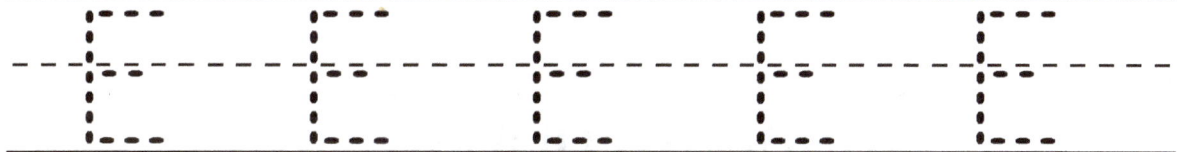

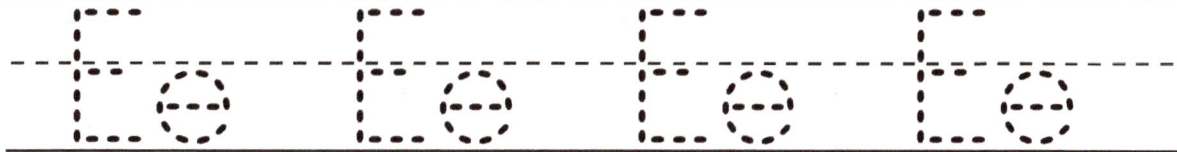

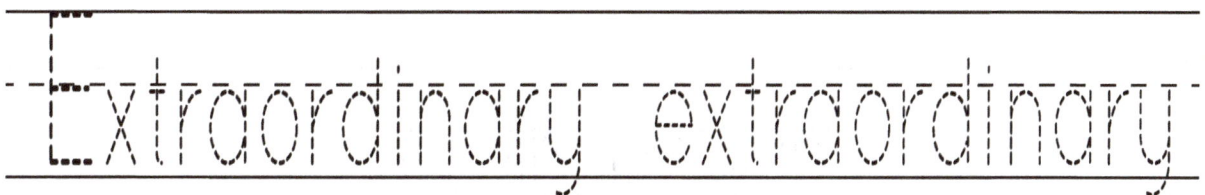

e e e e e

e e e e e

E E E E E

E E E E E

Ee Ee Ee Ee

Extraordinary extraordinary

Trace and Write.

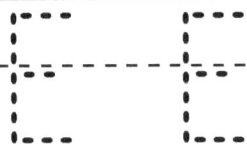

e   e

e

Practice writing a lowercase e.

Trace and Write.

E   E

E

Practice writing an uppercase E.

Trace.

I am extraordinary.

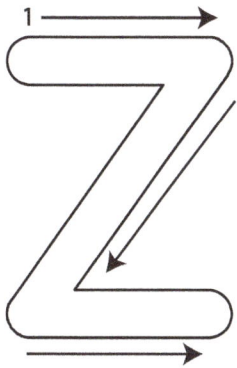

Z z

zebra

Trace and write.

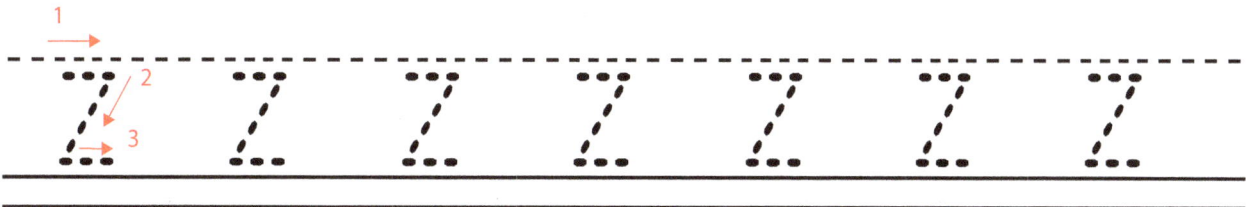

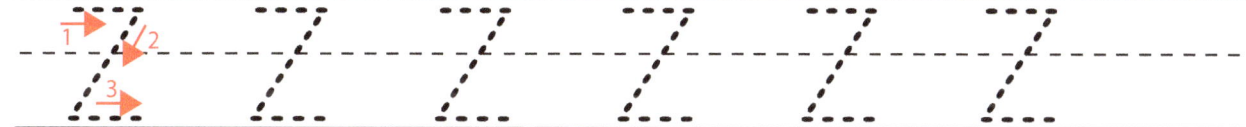

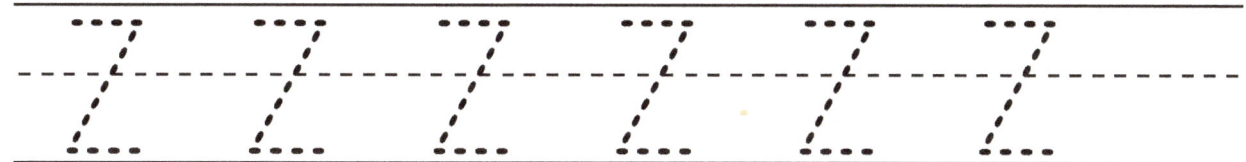

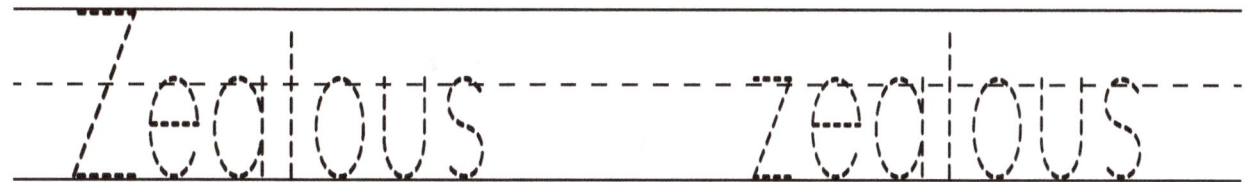

Z Z Z Z Z Z Z

Z Z Z Z Z Z Z

z z z z z z z

z z z z z z z

Zz Zz Zz Zz Zz

Zealous   Zealous

Trace and Write.

Z   Z

Z

Practice writing a lowercase z.

Trace and Write.

Z   Z

Z

Practice writing an uppercase Z.

Trace.

I am zealous !

Trace the letter for practice.

Aa Bb Cc Dd

Ee Ff Gg Hh

Ii Jj Kk Ll

Mm Nn Oo Pp

Qq Rr Ss Tt

Uu Vv Ww Xx

Yy Zz

Activity Pages

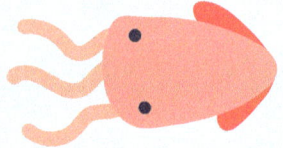

I AM AWESOME!

Color the pictures.

Put a circle around all the items beginning with the letter B.

I AM BRAVE!

CHICKEN MAZE

Help the chicken find a way to the chick.

I AM CREATIVE!

Circle the number that shows how many letter "D's" are in the picture.

7   8   9   2

I AM DYNAMIC!

Color the picture
using the crayon color key.

 **Blue** = **1**    **Red** = **2**

I AM EXTRAORDINARY!

Color the pictures.

Put a circle around all the items beginning
with the letter F.

I AM FOCUSED!

Circle the number that shows how many letter "G's" are in the picture.

2   6   9   8

I AM GREAT!

Color the pictures.

Put a circle around all the items beginning with the letter H.

I AM HELPFUL!

COLOR THE PICTURES.

Put a circle around all the items beginning
with the letter I.

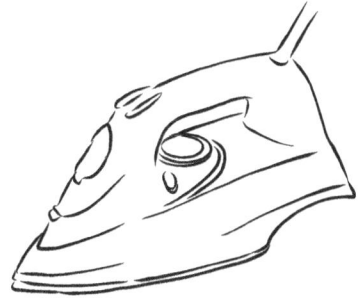

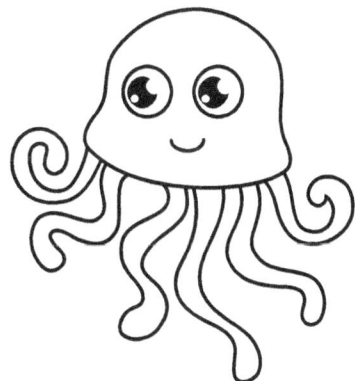

I AM INCREDIBLE!

Color the picture
using the crayon color key.

Black = 1   Orange = 2

Pink = 1   Yellow = 2

I AM JOYFUL!

COLOR THE PICTURES.

Put a circle around all the items beginning with the letter K.

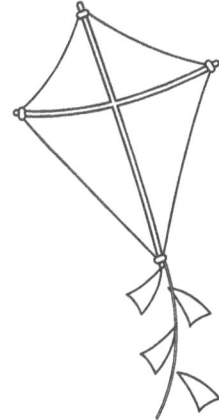

I AM KIND!

Color the picture
using the crayon color key.

Red = 1   Yellow = 2   Pink = 3

I AM A LEADER!

I AM MARVELOUS!

Bird Maze

Help the bird find a way to the hatchlings.

I AM NICE!

COLOR THE PICTURES.

Put a circle around all the items beginning with the letter O.

I AM OUTSTANDING!

Color the picture
using the crayon color key.

Blue = 1   Red = 2

I AM PHENOMENAL!

Circle the number that shows
how many letter "Q's" are in the picture.

8   5   7   3

I AM QUIRKY!

Color the pictures.

Put a circle around all the items beginning
with the letter R.

I AM RESPECTFUL!

I AM STRONG!

Color the pictures.

Put a circle around all the items beginning
with the letter T.

I AM TRUSTWORTHY!

Circle the number that shows how many letter "D's" are in the picture.

4   7   2   6

I AM UNIQUE!

Color the pictures.

Put a circle around all the items beginning
with the letter V.

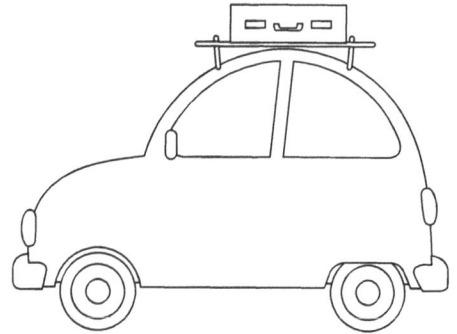

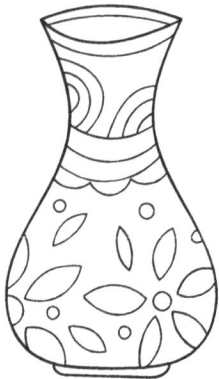

I AM VIBRANT!

I AM WORTHY!

Circle the number that shows how many letter "D's" are in the picture.

3 9 6 8

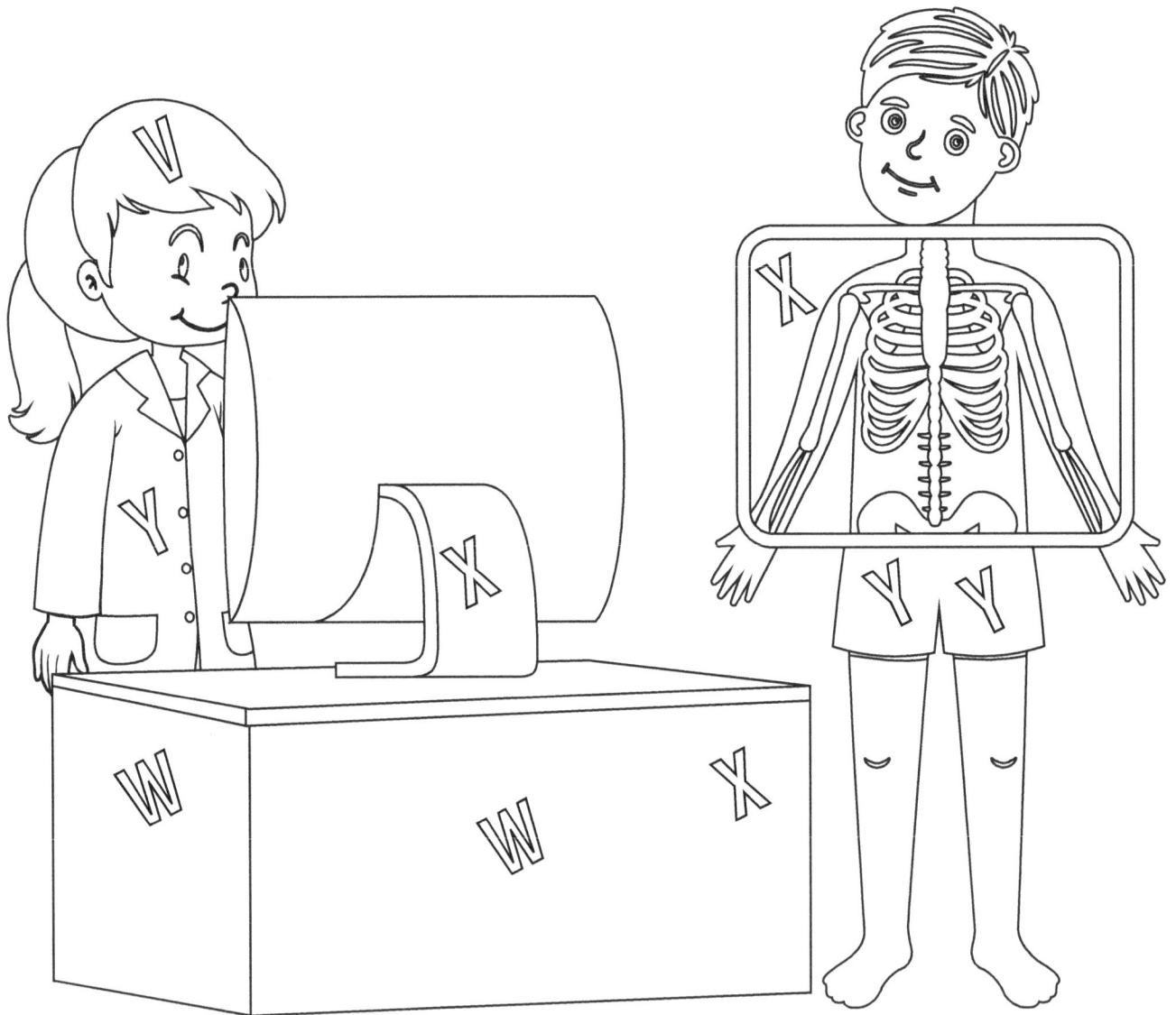

I AM A X-FACTOR!

Color the picture
using the crayon color key.

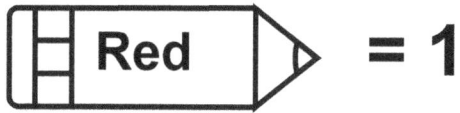

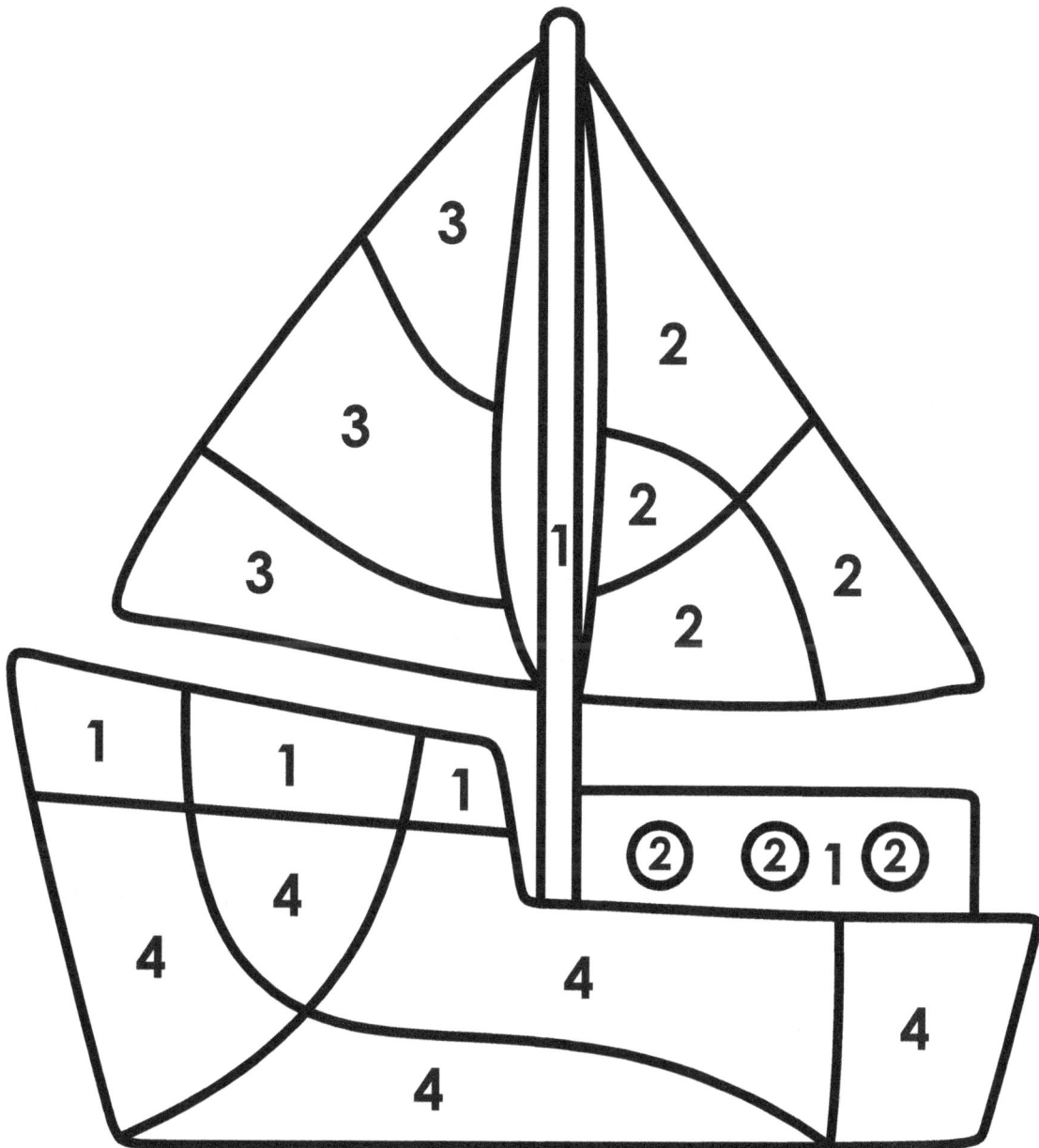

Gray = 1

Blue = 2

Red = 1

Yellow = 2

3

2

3

2

3

2

1

2

2

1

1

1

② ② 1 ②

4

4

4

4

4

4

I AM YOUTHFUL!

ZOO

I AM ZEALOUS!

Select an affirmation each day to read and memorize to encourage you to believe in yourself.

I am awesome!

I am brave!

I am creative!

I am dynamic!

I am extraordinary!

I am focused!

I am great!

I am helpful!

I am incredible!

I am joyful!

I am kind!

I am a leader!

I am marvelous!

I am nice!

I am outstanding!

I am phenomenal!

I am quirky!

I am respectful!

I am strong!

I am trustworthy!

I am unique!

I am vibrant!

I am worthy!

I am a x-factor!

I am youthful!

I am zealous!

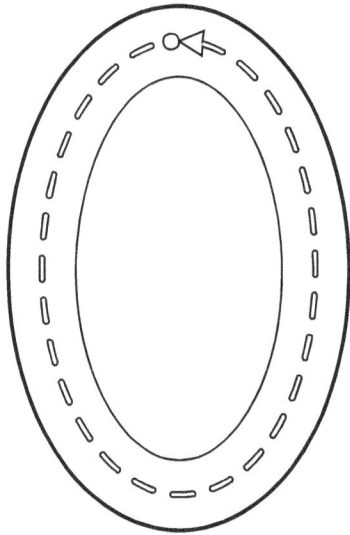

0 Zero

Trace and practice writing the number.

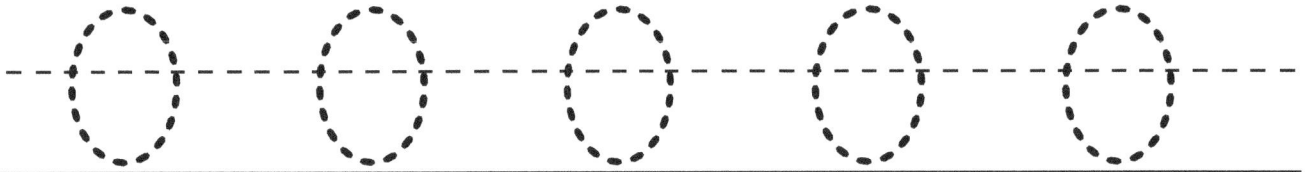

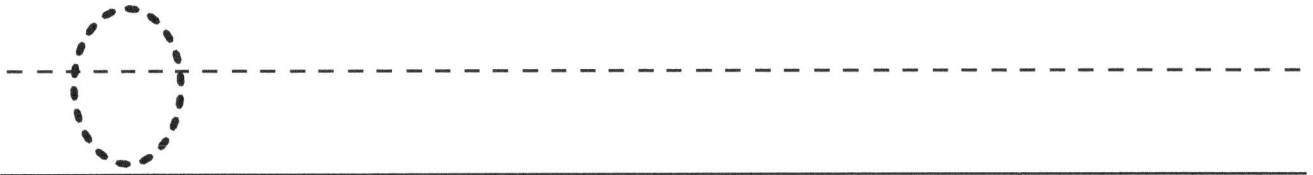

0 0 0 0 0

0

Trace and practice writing the number word.

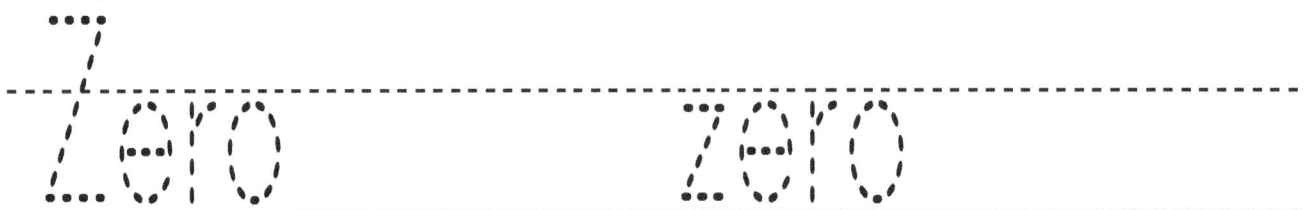

Zero Zero zero zero

Zero zero

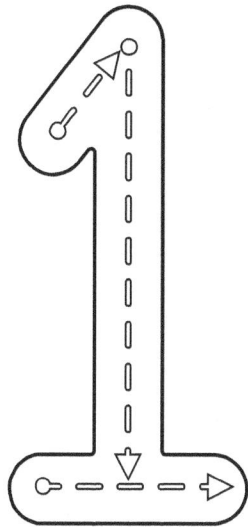

1

One

Trace and practice writing the number.

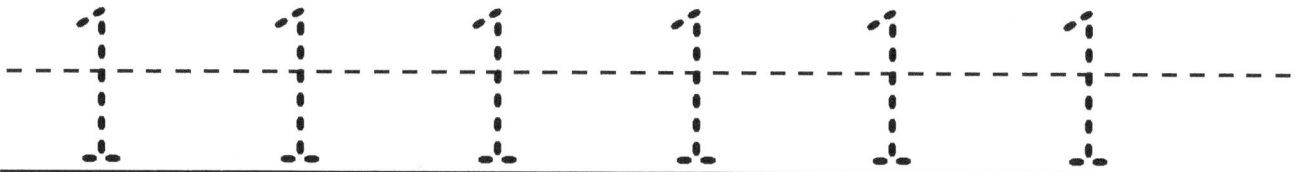

1 1 1 1 1 1

1

Trace and practice writing the number word.

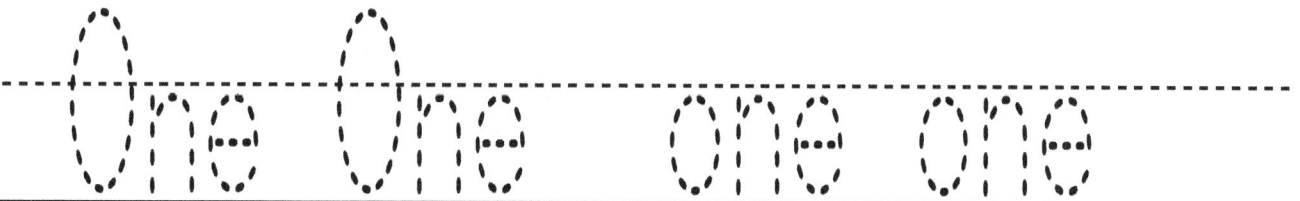

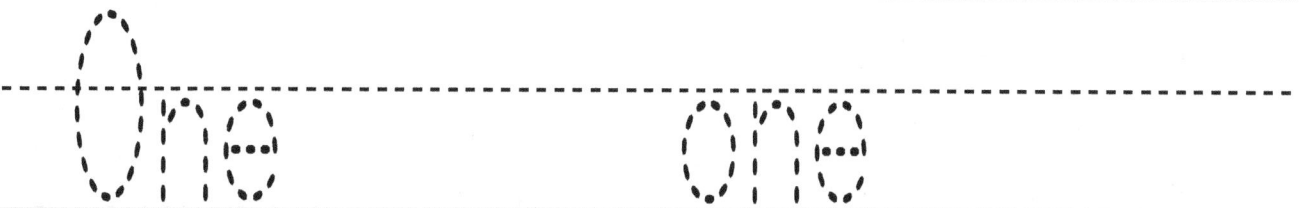

One One one one

One one

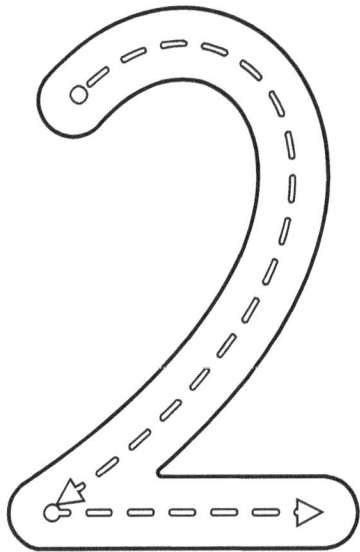

2   Two

Trace and practice writing the number.

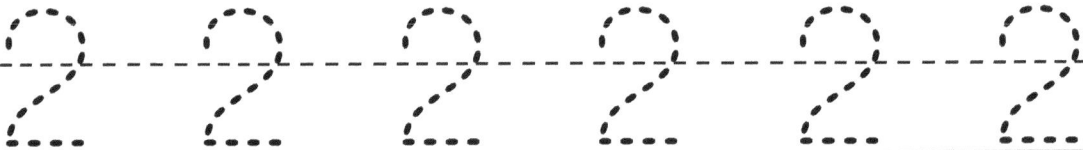

2 2 2 2 2 2

2

Trace and practice writing the number word.

Two Two Two Two

Two Two

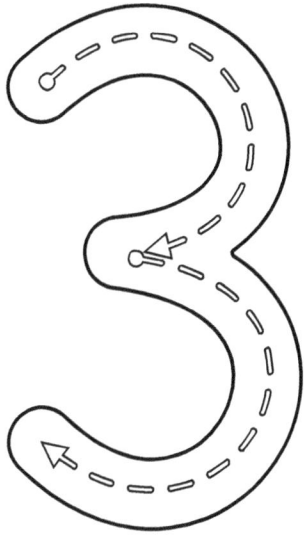

3 Three

Trace and practice writing the number.

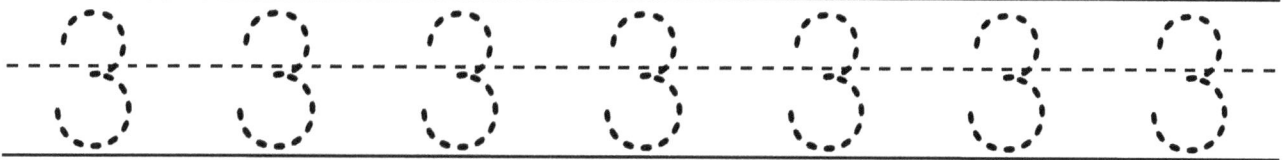

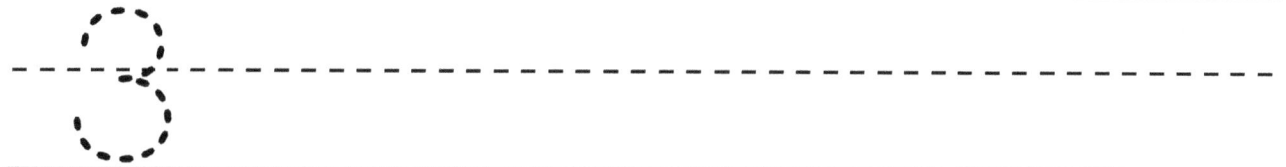

3 3 3 3 3 3 3

3

Trace and practice writing the number word.

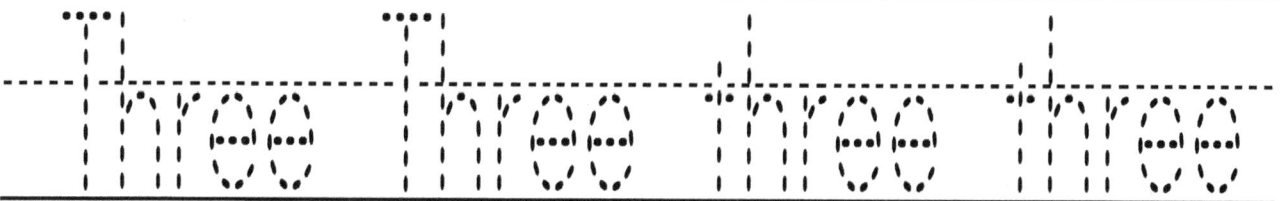

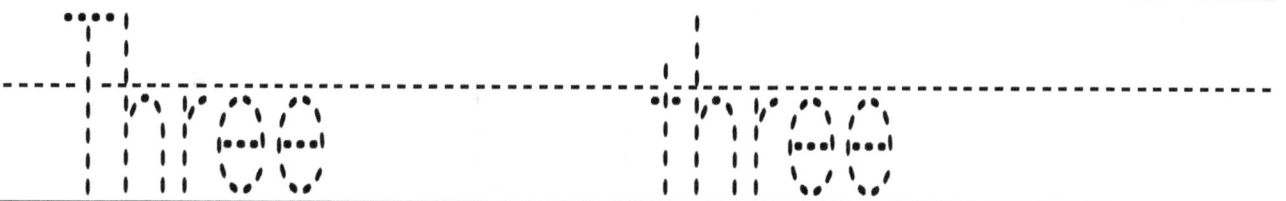

Three Three three three

Three three

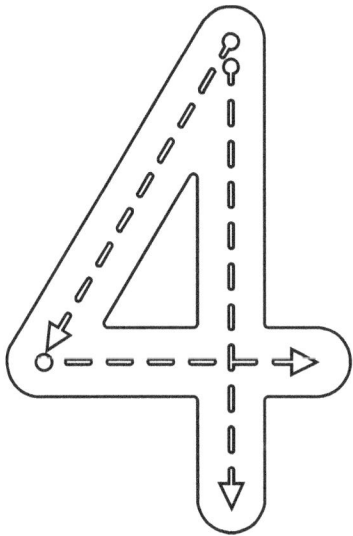

4 **Four**

Trace and practice writing the number.

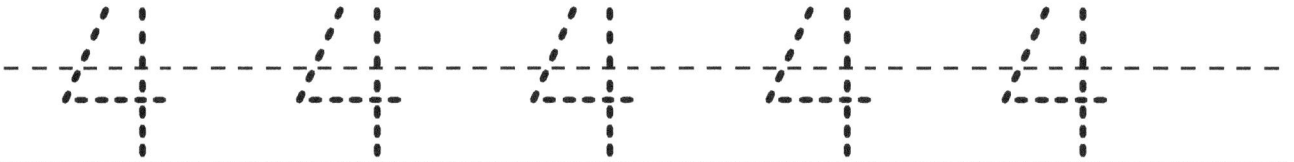

4 4 4 4 4

4

Trace and practice writing the number word.

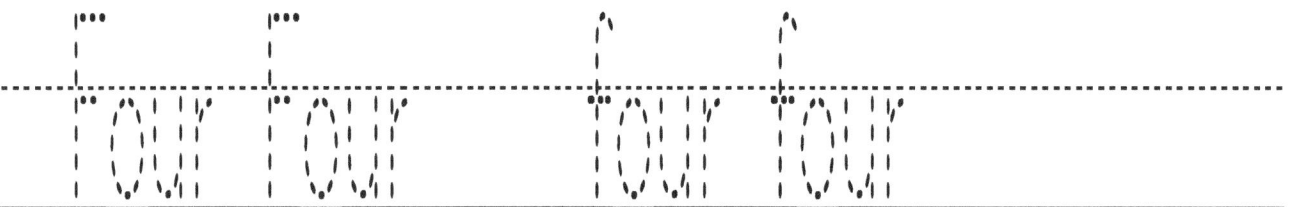

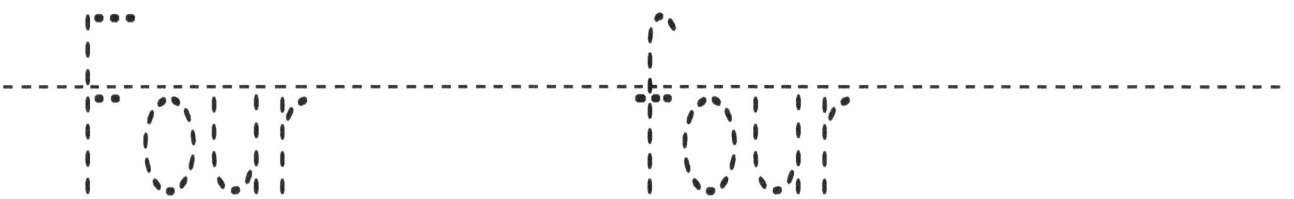

four four four four

Four four

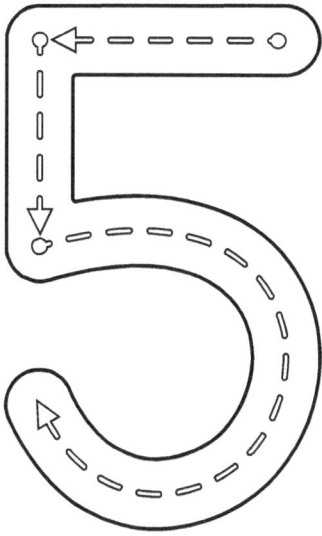

5 Five

Trace and practice writing the number.

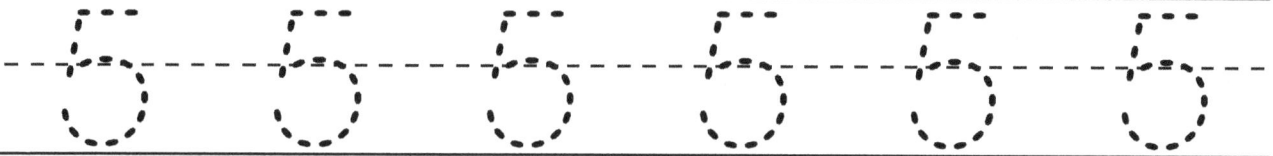

5 5 5 5 5 5

5

Trace and practice writing the number word.

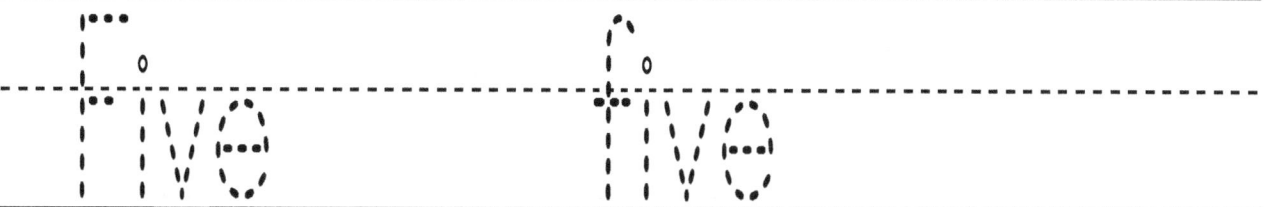

five five five five

Five five

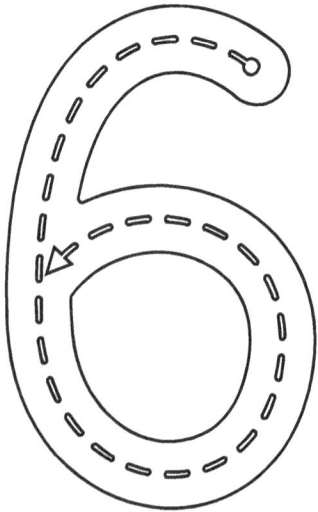

6

Six

Trace and practice writing the number.

6 6 6 6 6 6 6

6

Trace and practice writing the number word.

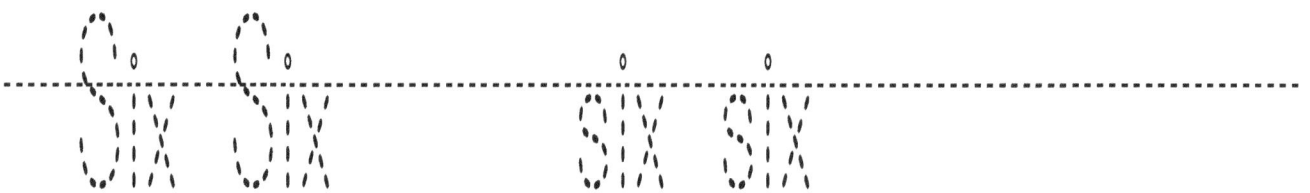

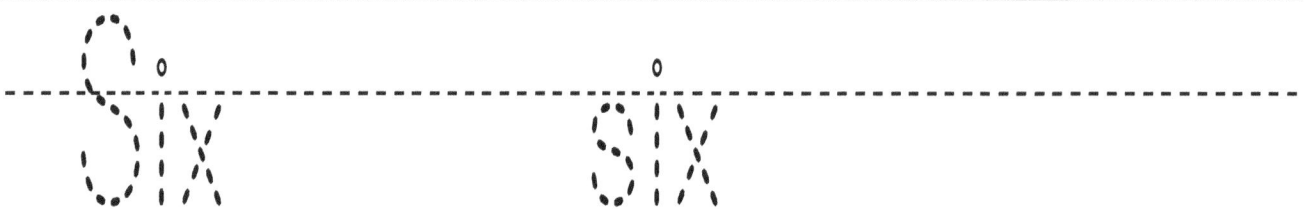

Six Six six six

Six six

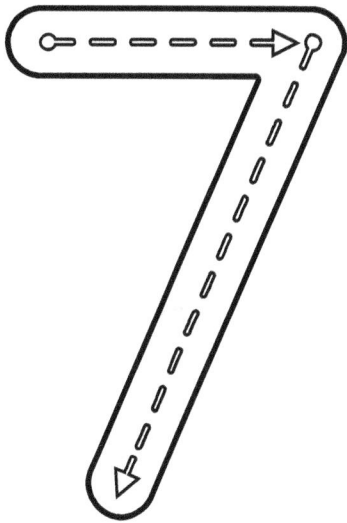

7 Seven

Trace and practice writing the number.

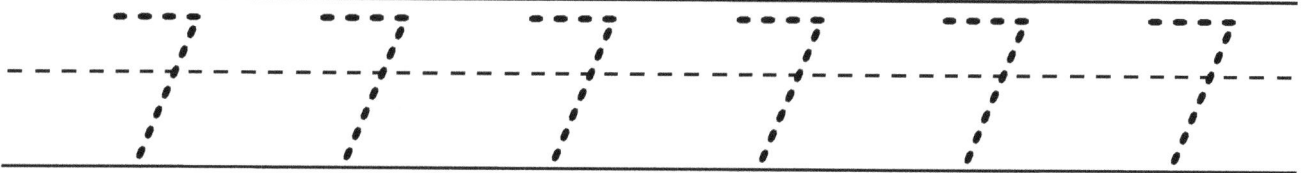

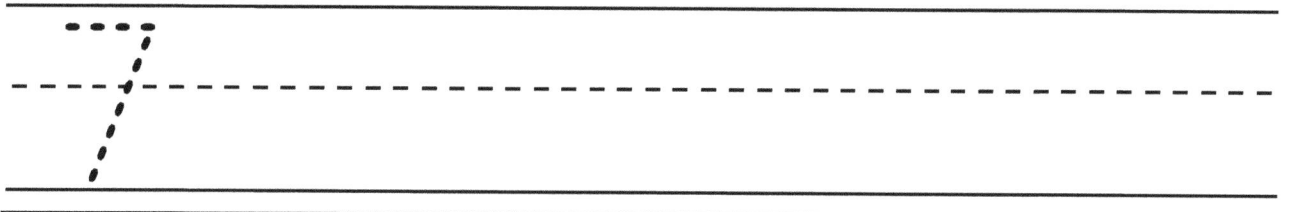

7 7 7 7 7 7

7

Trace and practice writing the number word.

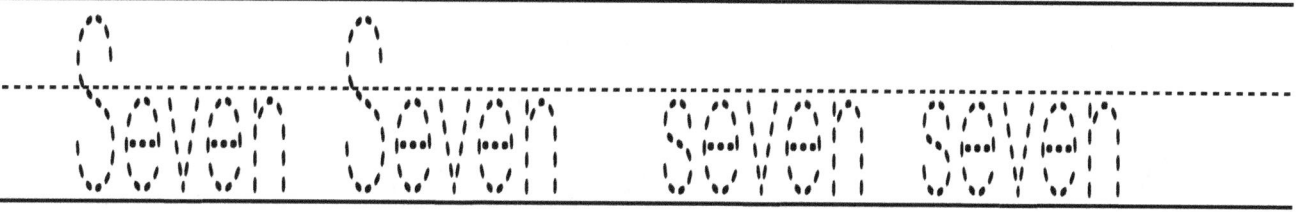

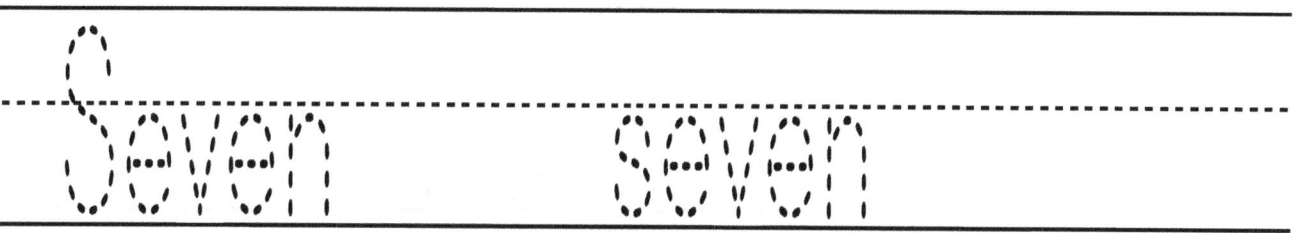

Seven Seven seven seven

Seven seven

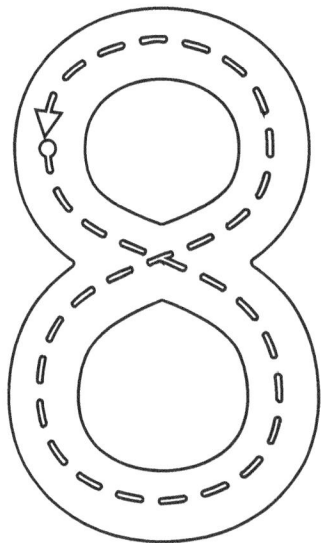

8   Eight

Trace and practice writing the number.

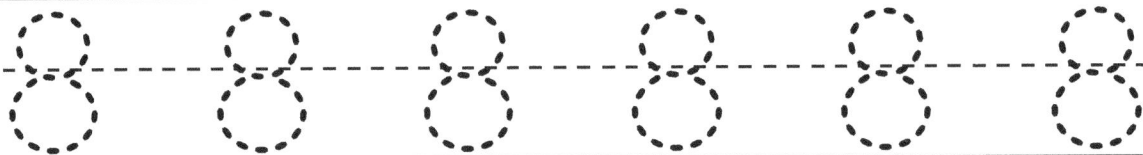

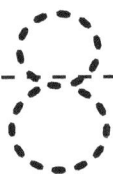

8 8 8 8 8 8

8

Trace and practice writing the number word.

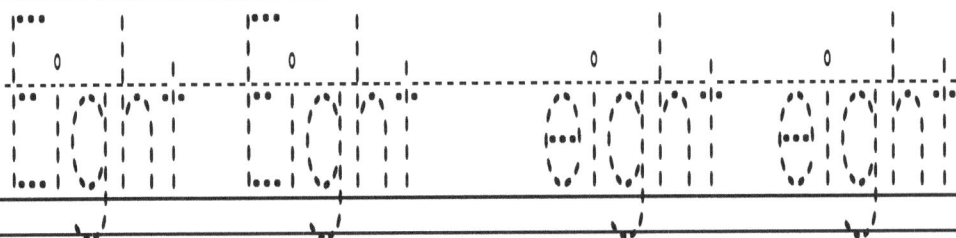

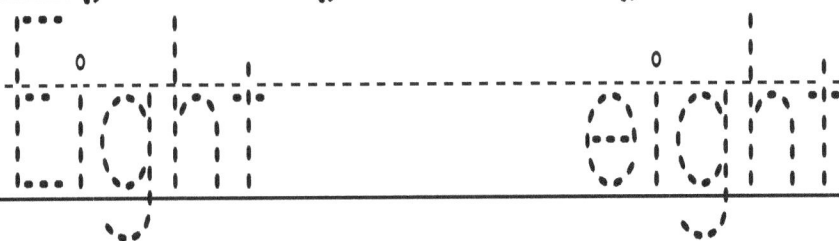

Eight Eight   eight eight

Eight   eight

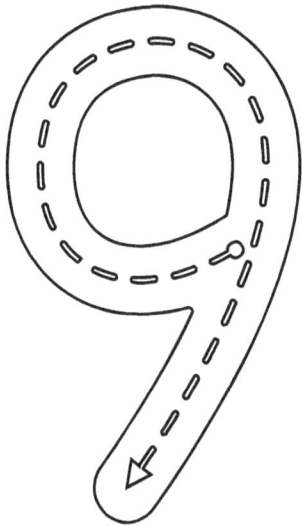

9 Nine

Trace and practice writing the number.

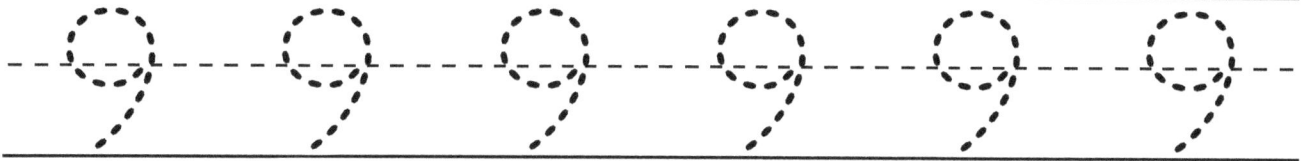

9 9 9 9 9 9

9

Trace and practice writing the number word.

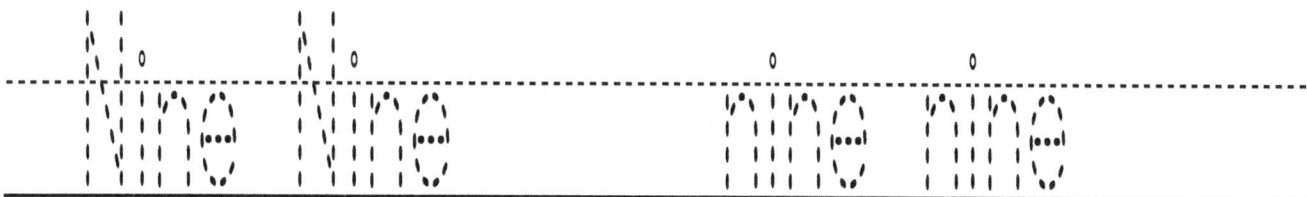

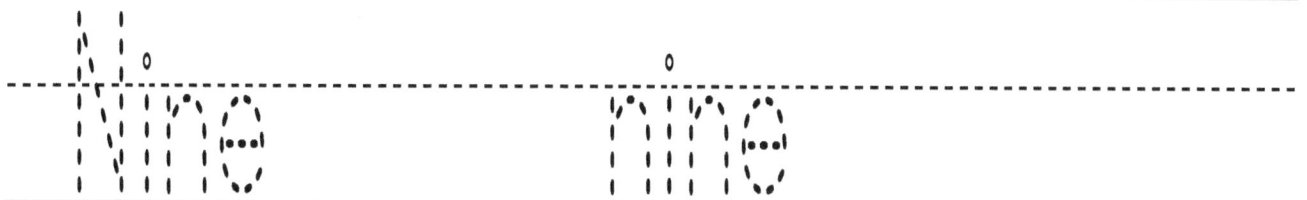

Nine Nine nine nine

Nine nine

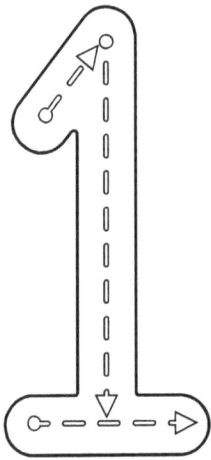

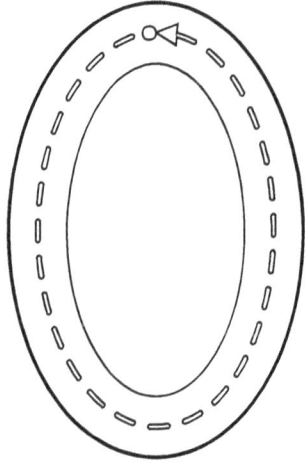

10 Ten

Trace and practice writing the number.

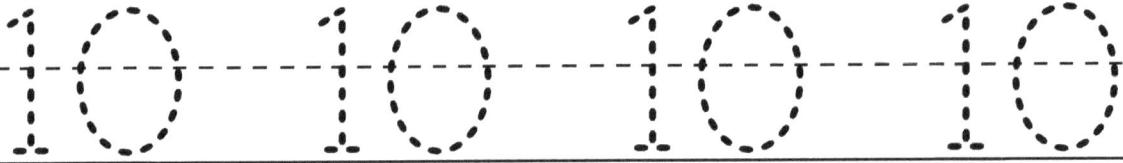

10 10 10 10

10

Trace and practice writing the number word.

Ten Ten ten ten

Ten ten

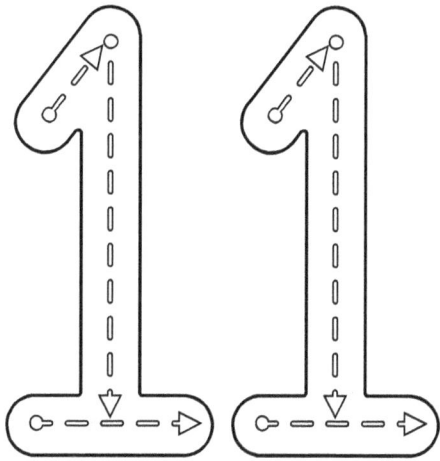

11 Eleven

Trace and practice writing the number.

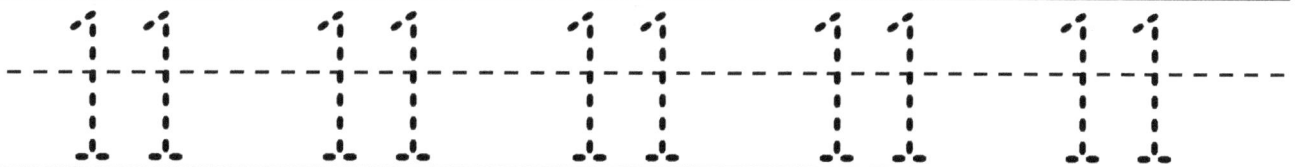

11 11 11 11 11

11

Trace and practice writing the number word.

Eleven Eleven   eleven eleven

Eleven   eleven

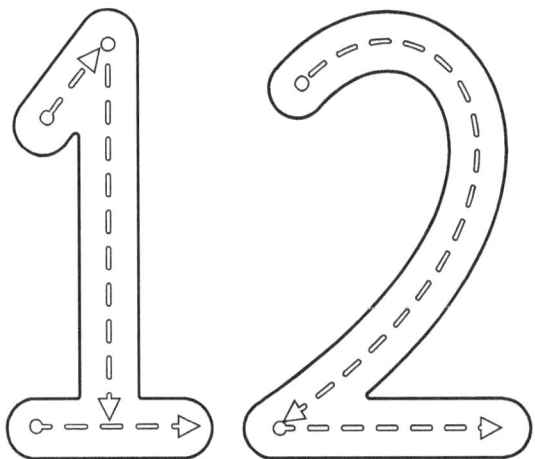

12 Twelve

Trace and practice writing the number.

12 12 12 12 12

12

Trace and practice writing the number word.

Twelve Twelve Twelve Twelve

Twelve twelve

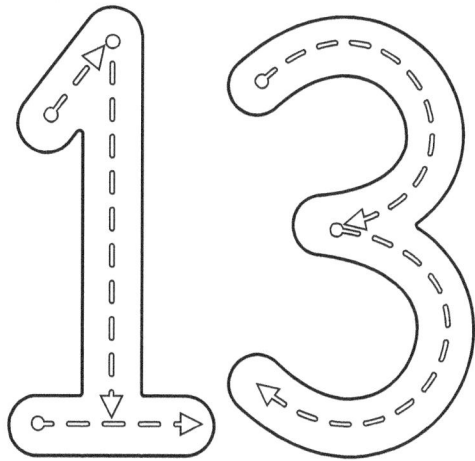

13 Thirteen

Trace and practice writing the number.

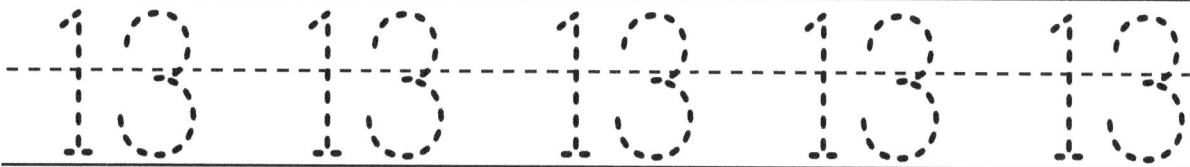

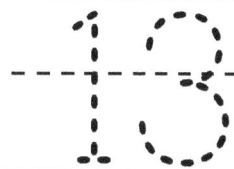

13   13   13   13   13

13

Trace and practice writing the number word.

Thirteen   Thirteen   thirteen   thirteen

Thirteen   thirteen

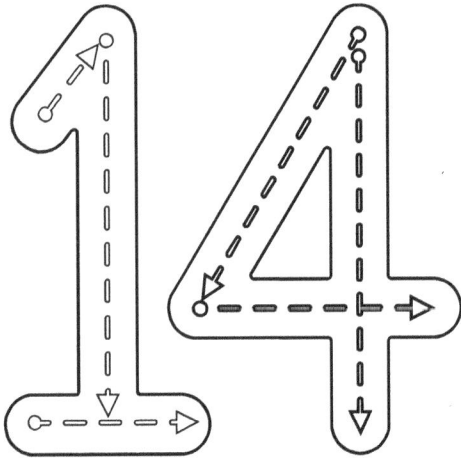

14 Fourteen

Trace and practice writing the number.

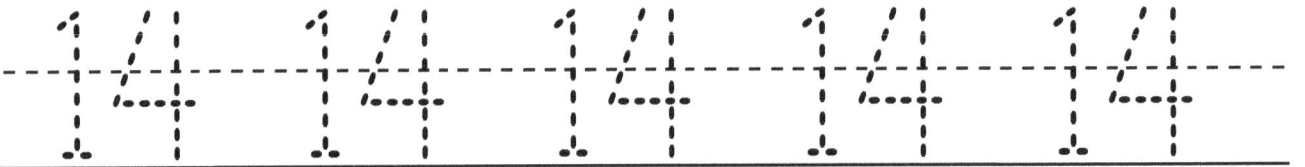

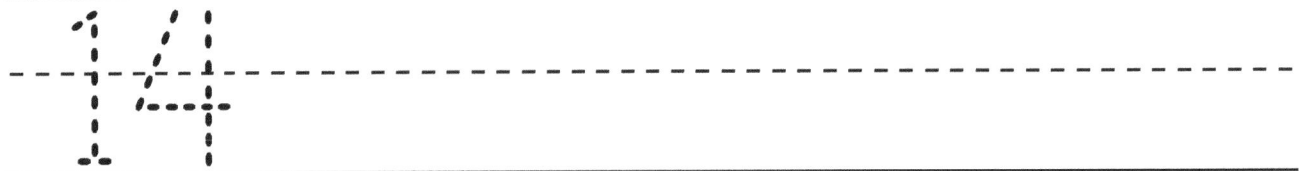

14 14 14 14 14

14

Trace and practice writing the number word.

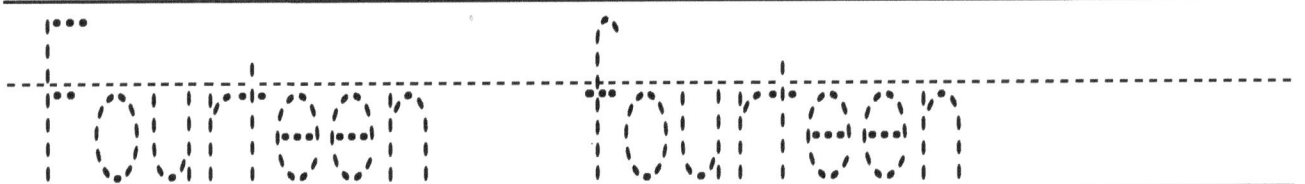

fourteen fourteen fourteen fourteen

Fourteen fourteen

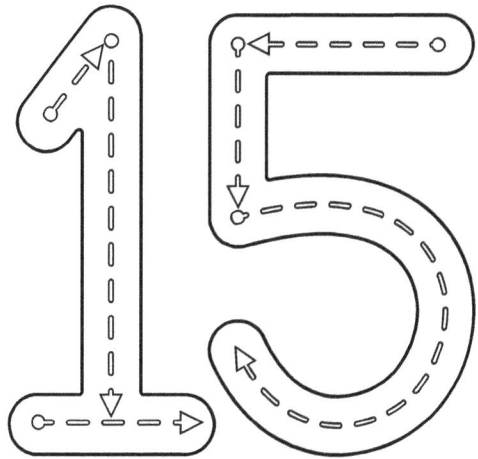

15 Fifteen

Trace and practice writing the number.

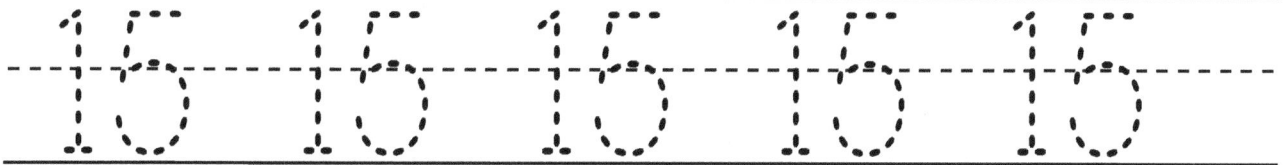

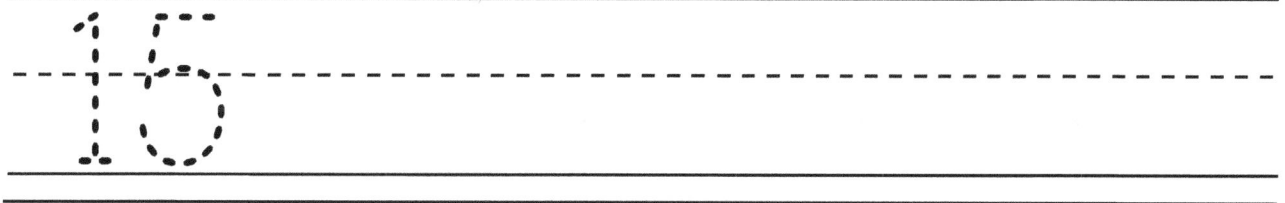

15 15 15 15 15

15

Trace and practice writing the number word.

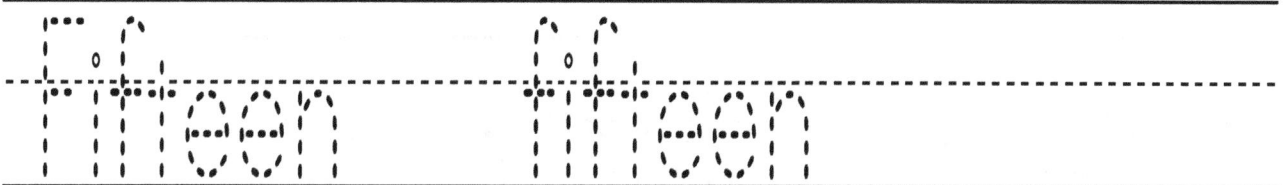

fifteen fifteen fifteen fifteen

Fifteen fifteen

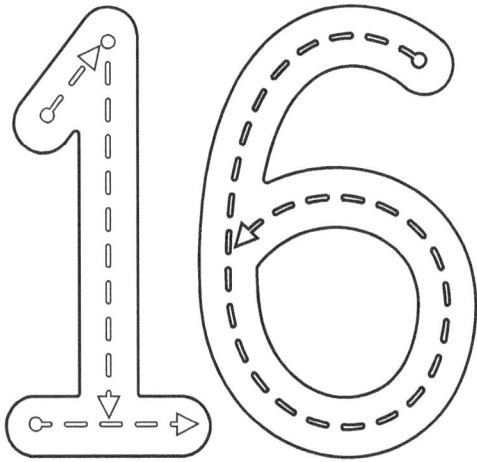

16 Sixteen

Trace and practice writing the number.

16 16 16 16 16

16

Trace and practice writing the number word.

Sixteen Sixteen sixteen sixteen

Sixteen sixteen

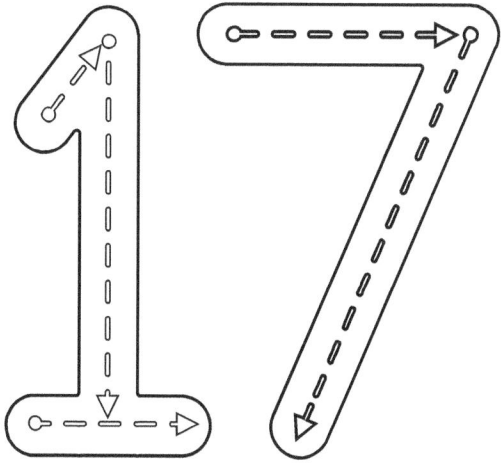

17 Seventeen

Trace and practice writing the number.

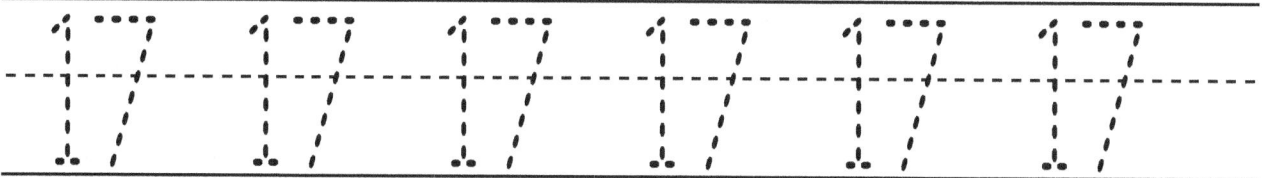

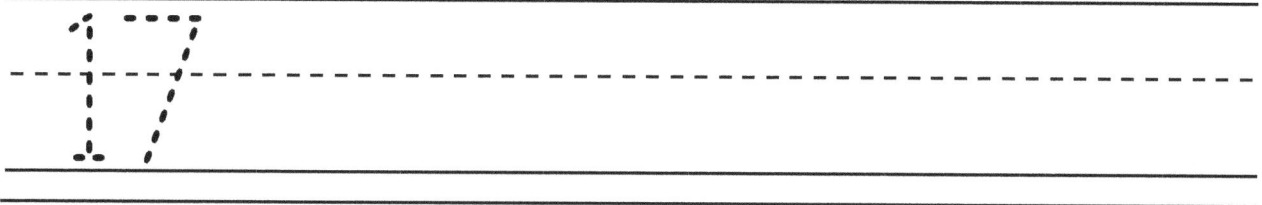

17 17 17 17 17 17

17

Trace and practice writing the number word.

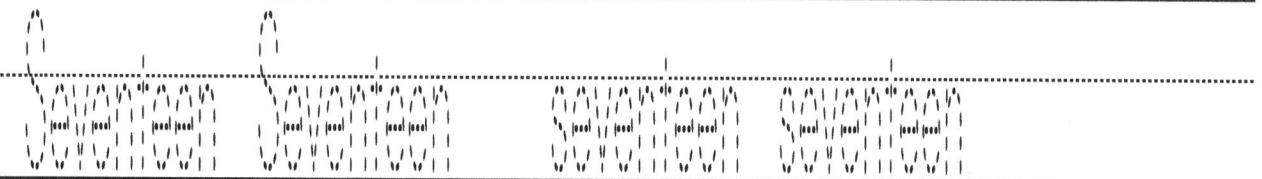

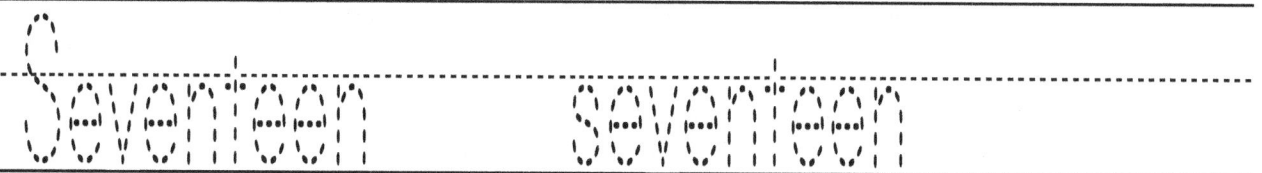

seventeen seventeen seventeen seventeen

Seventeen seventeen

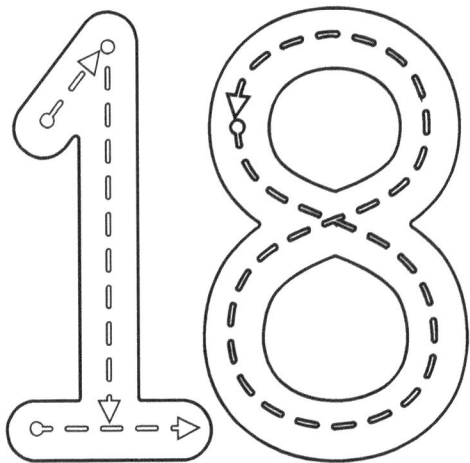

18 Eighteen

Trace and practice writing the number.

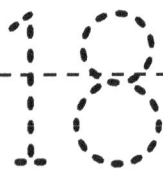

18 18 18 18 18 18

18

Trace and practice writing the number word.

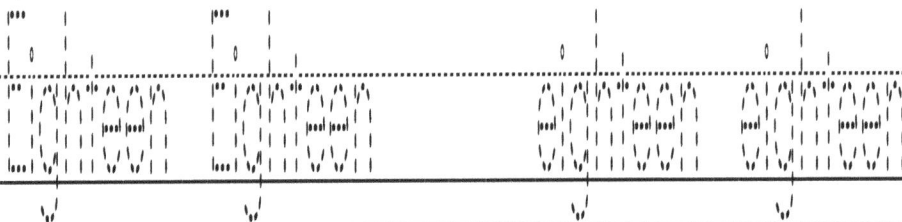

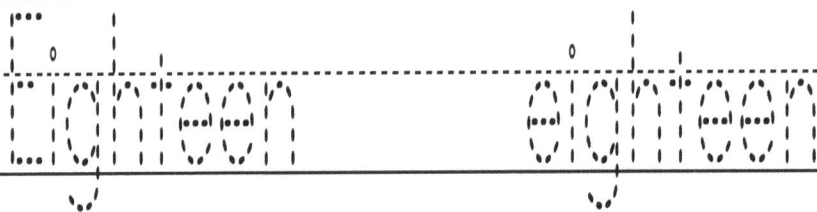

eighteen eighteen eighteen eighteen

Eighteen eighteen

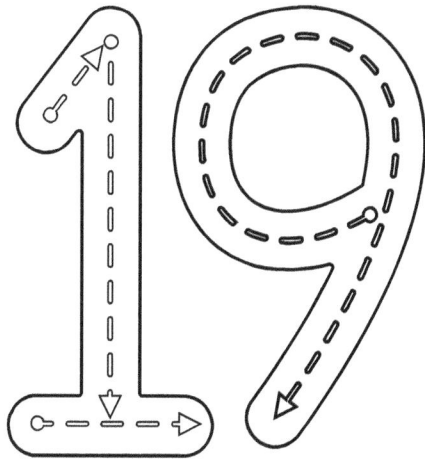

19 Nineteen

Trace and practice writing the number.

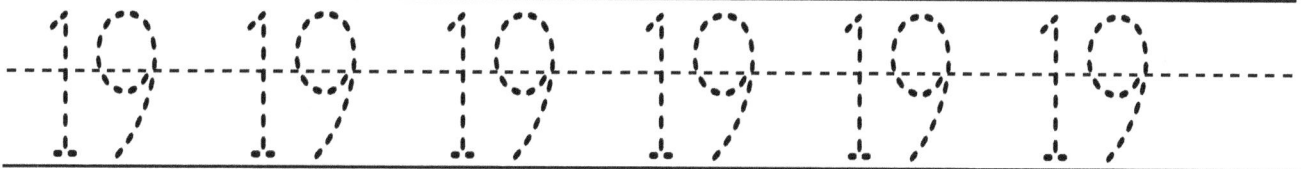

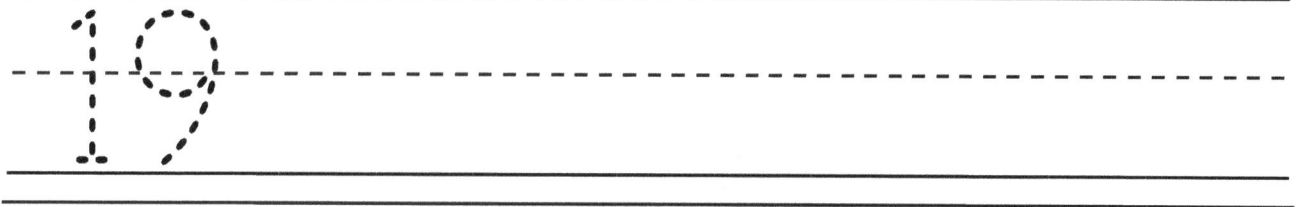

19 19 19 19 19 19

19

Trace and practice writing the number word.

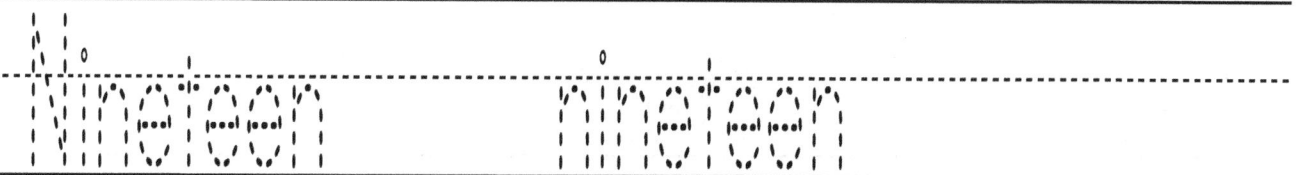

Nineteen nineteen nineteen nineteen

Nineteen nineteen

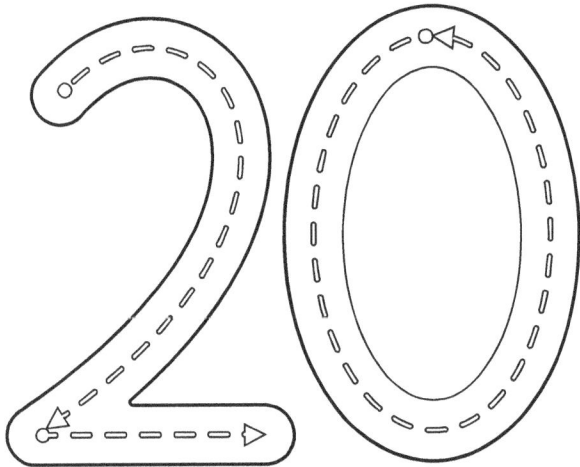

20 Twenty

Trace and practice writing the number.

20 20 20 20 20

20

Trace and practice writing the number word.

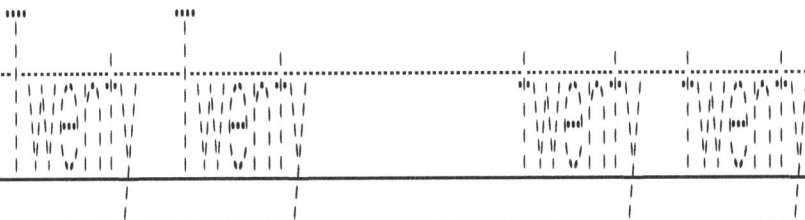

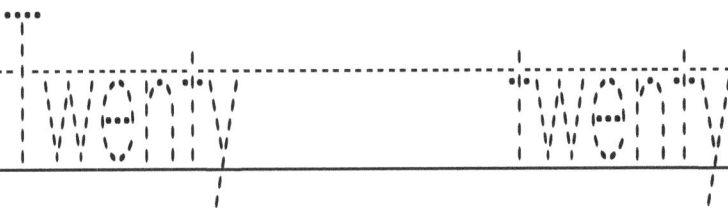

Twenty Twenty Twenty

Twenty   Twenty

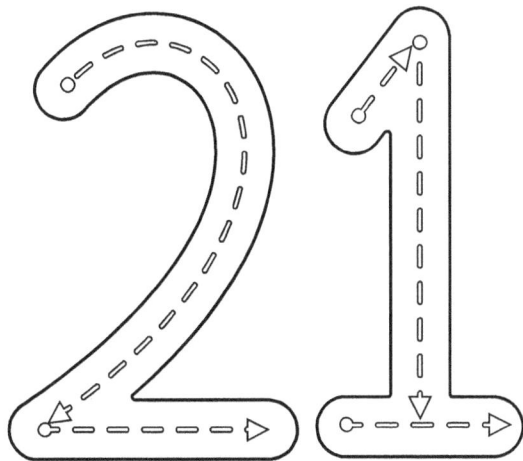

21 Twenty-one

Trace and practice writing the number.

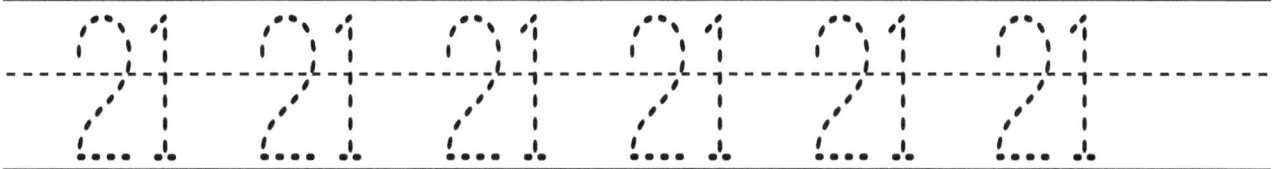

21 21 21 21 21 21

21

Trace and practice writing the number word.

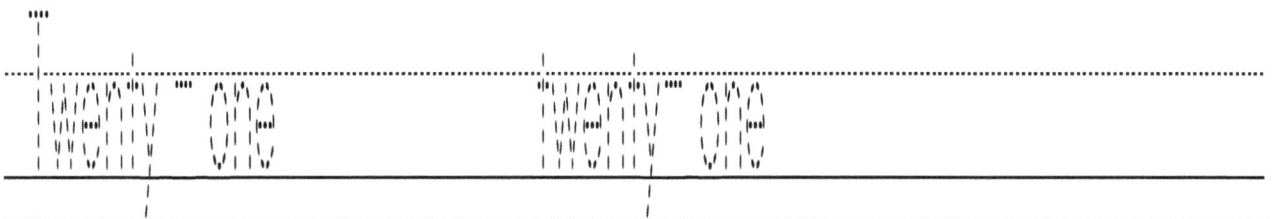

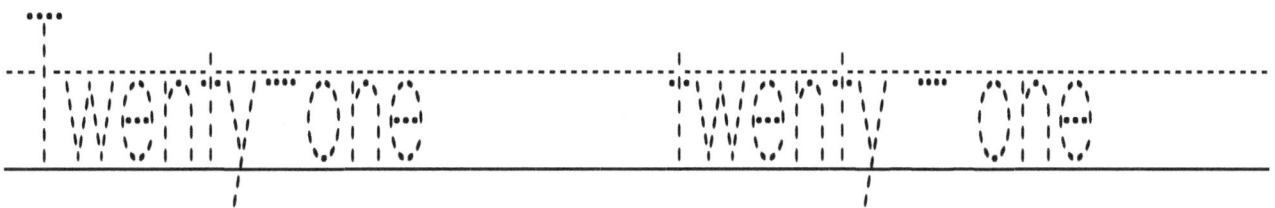

twenty one   twenty one

Twenty one   Twenty one

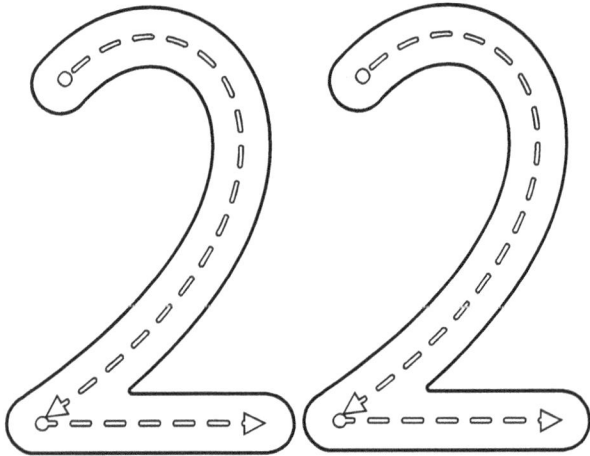

22 Twenty-two

Trace and practice writing the number.

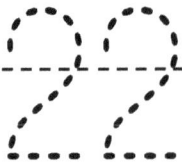

22 22 22 22 22 22

22

Trace and practice writing the number word.

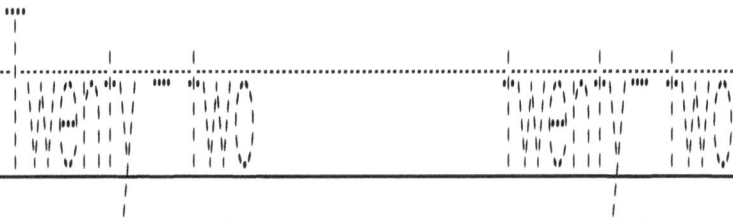

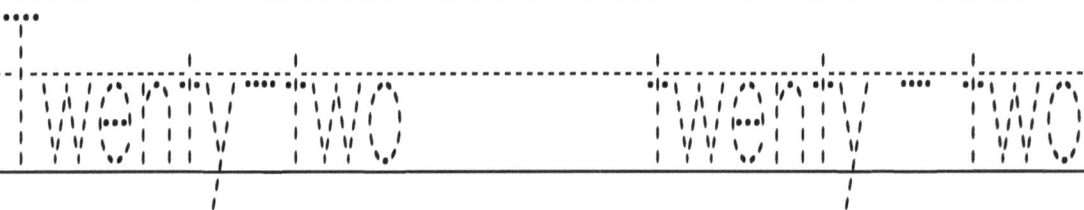

twenty two   twenty two

Twenty two   twenty two

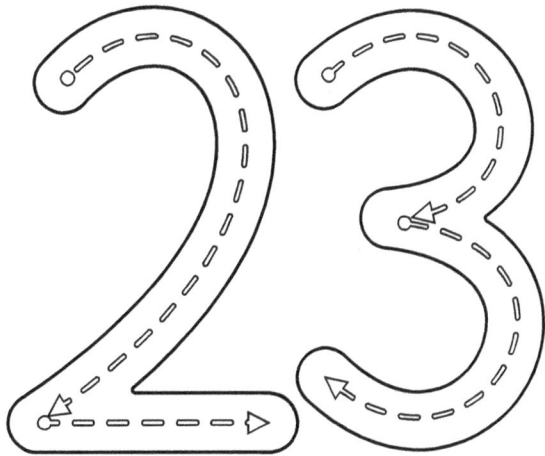

23 Twenty-three

Trace and practice writing the number.

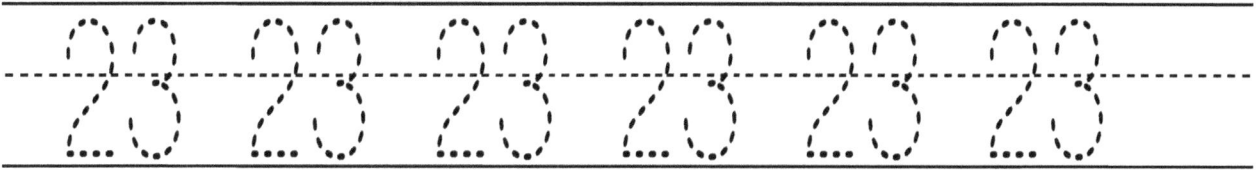

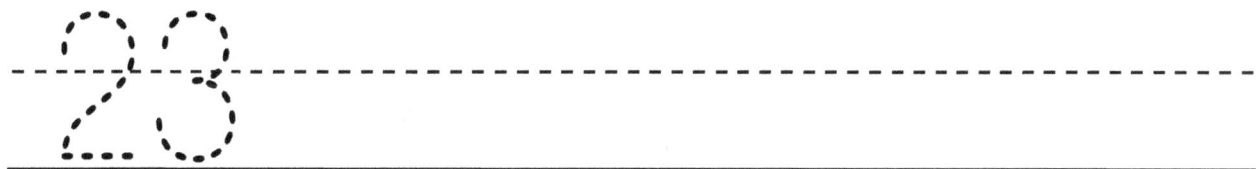

23 23 23 23 23 23

23

Trace and practice writing the number word.

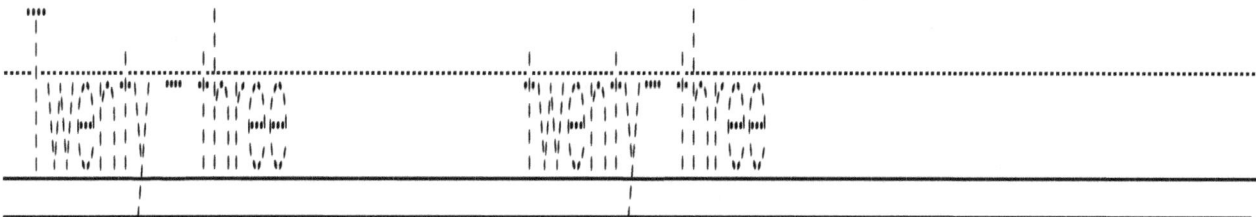

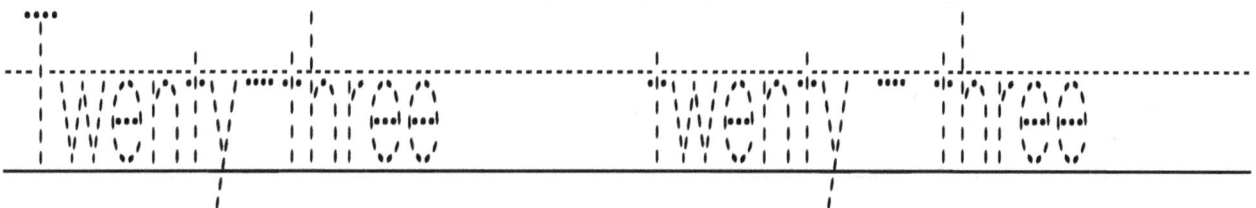

twenty-two twenty-two

Twenty-three twenty-three

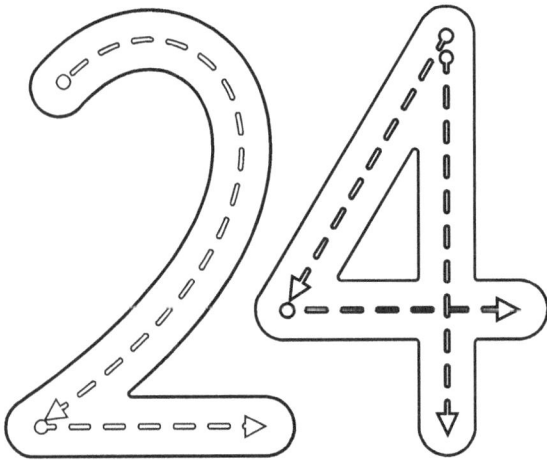

24 Twenty-four

Trace and practice writing the number.

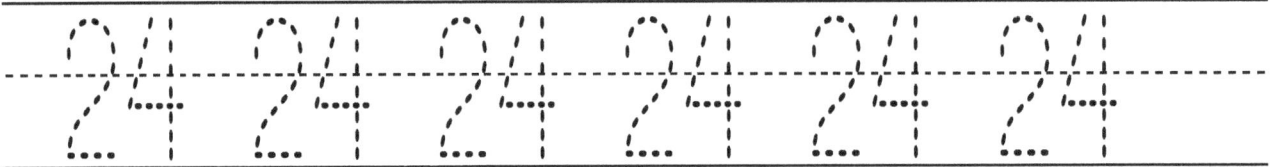

24 24 24 24 24 24

24

Trace and practice writing the number word.

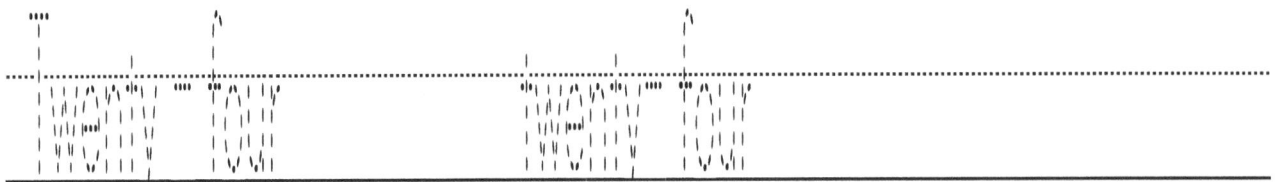

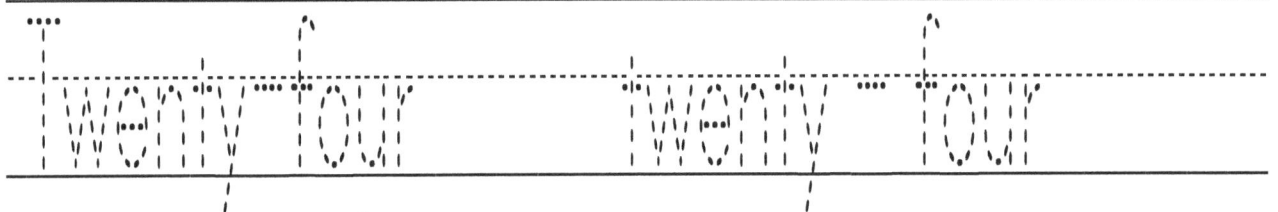

Twenty four   Twenty four

Twenty-four   twenty four

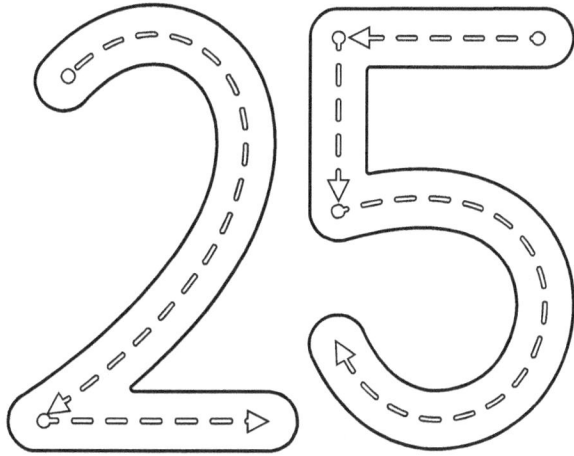

25 Twenty-five

Trace and practice writing the number.

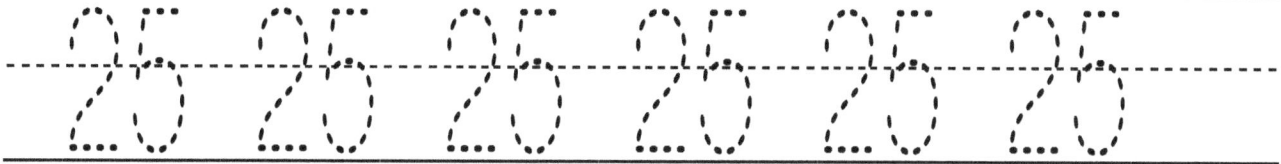

25 25 25 25 25 25

25

Trace and practice writing the number word.

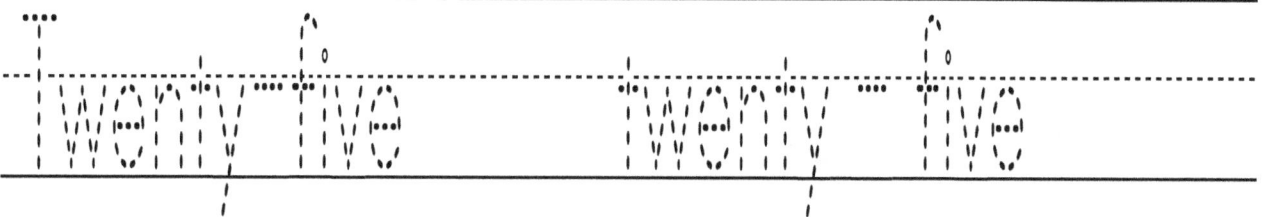

twenty two   twenty two

Twenty-five   twenty-five

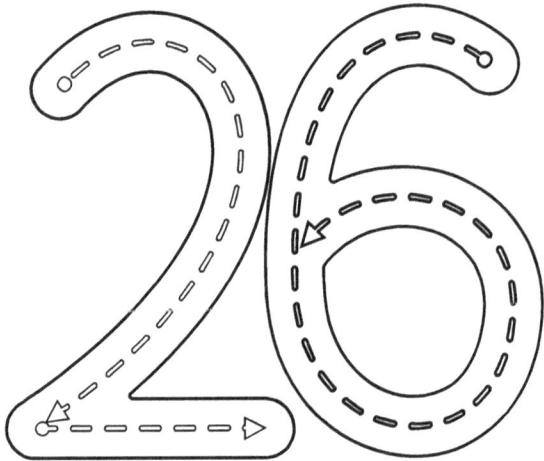

26 Twenty- six

Trace and practice writing the number.

26 26 26 26 26 26

26

Trace and practice writing the number word.

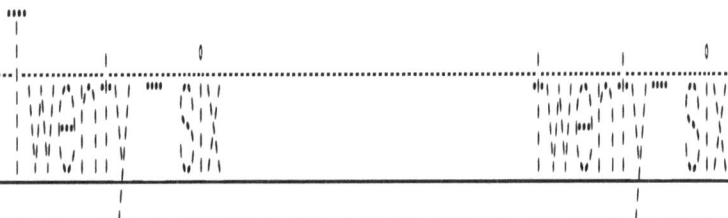

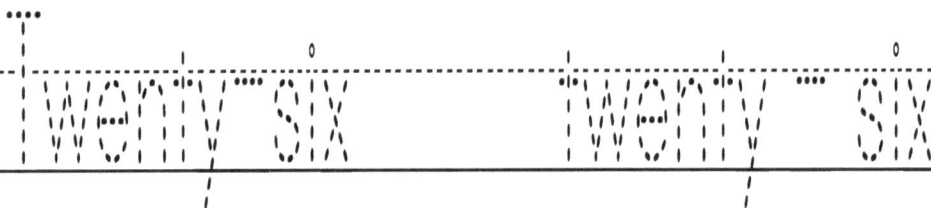

twenty six   twenty six

Twenty six   twenty six

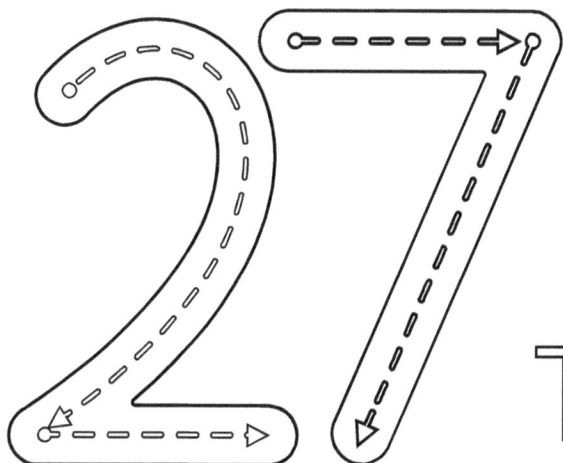

27 Twenty-seven

Trace and practice writing the number.

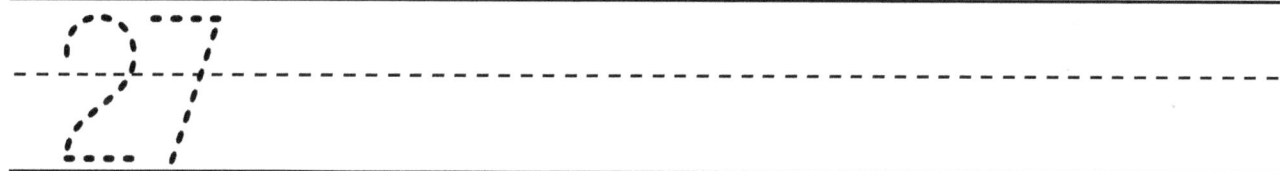

27 27 27 27 27 27 27 27 27 27 27 27

27

Trace and practice writing the number word.

twenty seven   twenty seven

twenty seven   twenty seven

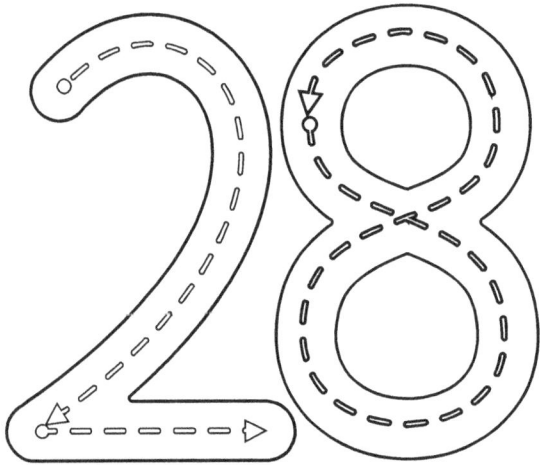

28 Twenty-eight

Trace and practice writing the number.

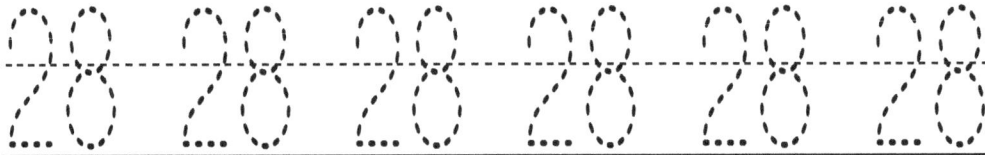

28 28 28 28 28 28

28

Trace and practice writing the number word.

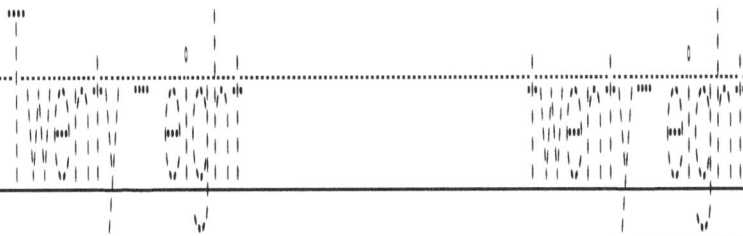

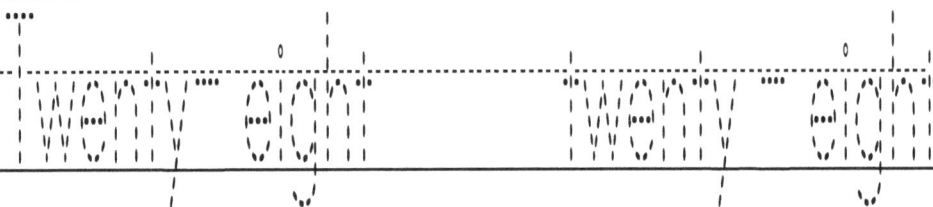

twenty eight   twenty eight

twenty eight   twenty eight

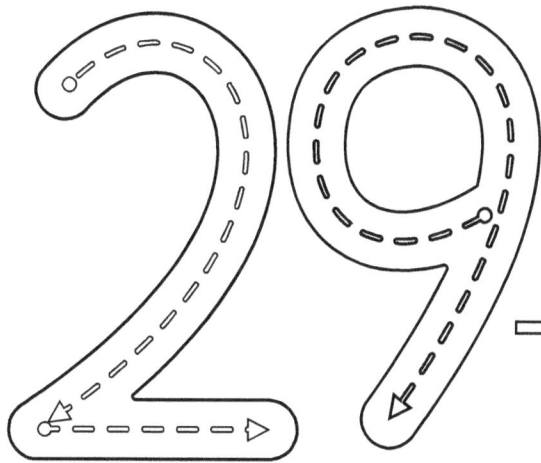

29 Twenty-nine

Trace and practice writing the number.

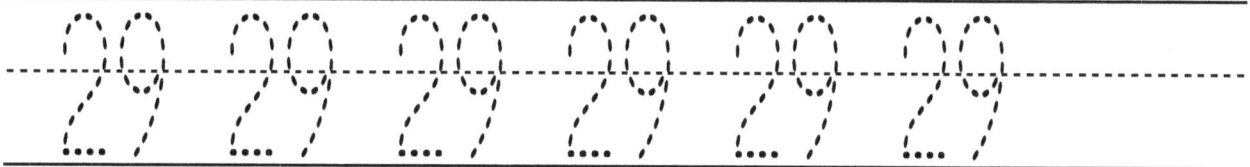

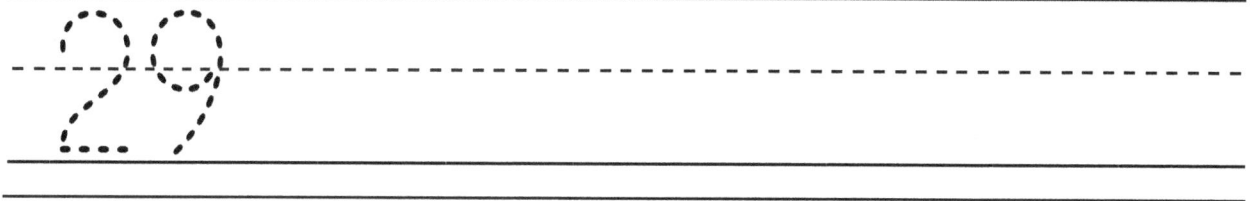

29 29 29 29 29 29

29

Trace and practice writing the number word.

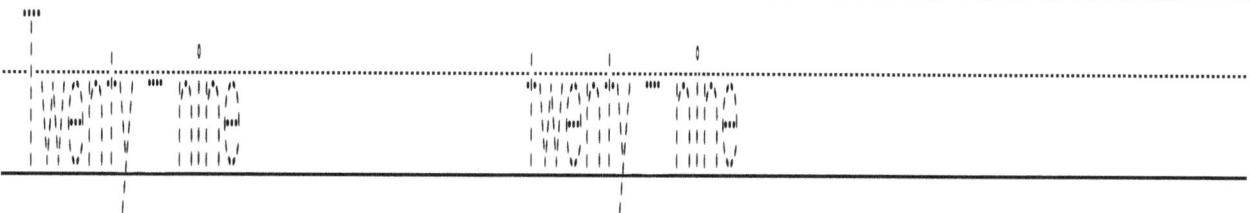

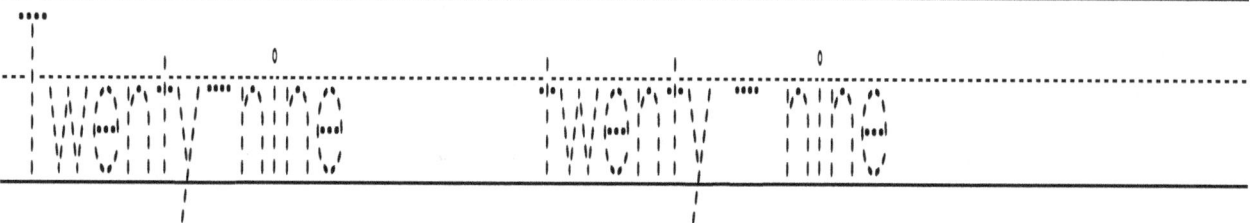

twenty nine   twenty nine

twenty-nine   twenty-nine

30 Thirty

Trace and practice writing the number.

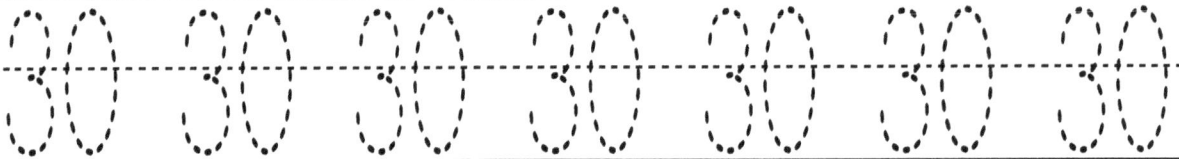

30 30 30 30 30 30 30

30

Trace and practice writing the number word.

Thirty

Thirty

0 Zero

Color each star with the number 0.

1   4   0   0

6

2   3   0

0   8   5   0

0 1 2 3 4 5 6 7 8 9 10 11 12 13 14 15 16 17 18 19 20 21 22 23 24 25 26 27 28 29 30

1 One

Color each half moon with the number 1.

Count and color one drum.

0 1 2 3 4 5 6 7 8 9 10 11 12 13 14 15 16 17 18 19 20 21 22 23 24 25 26 27 28 29 30

2 Two

Color each heart with the number 2.

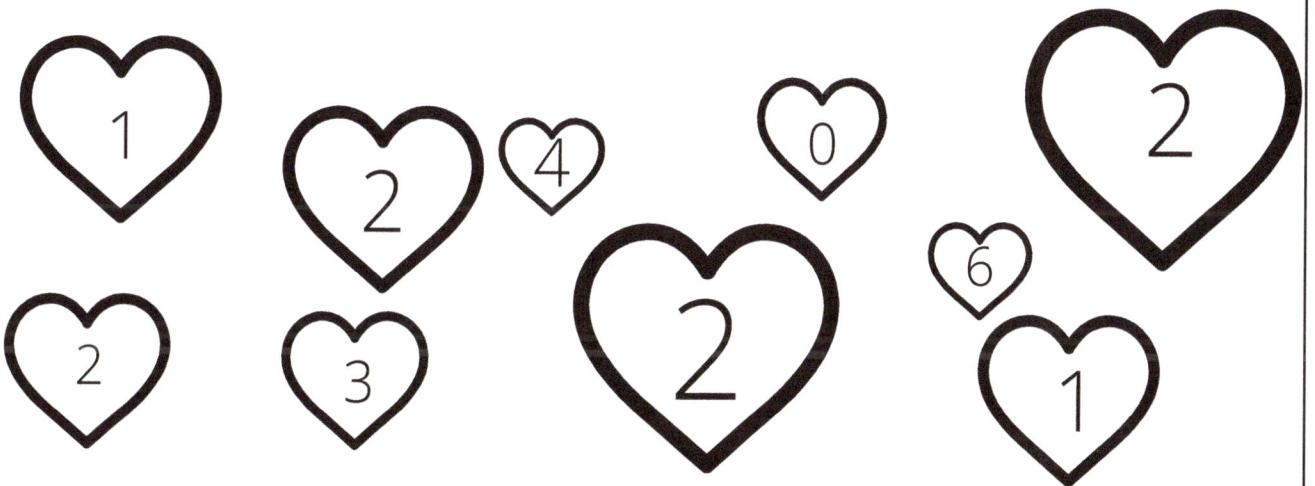

Count and color two teddy bears.

0 1 2 3 4 5 6 7 8 9 10 11 12 13 14 15 16 17 18 19 20 21 22 23 24 25 26 27 28 29 30

3 Three

Color each circle with the number 3.

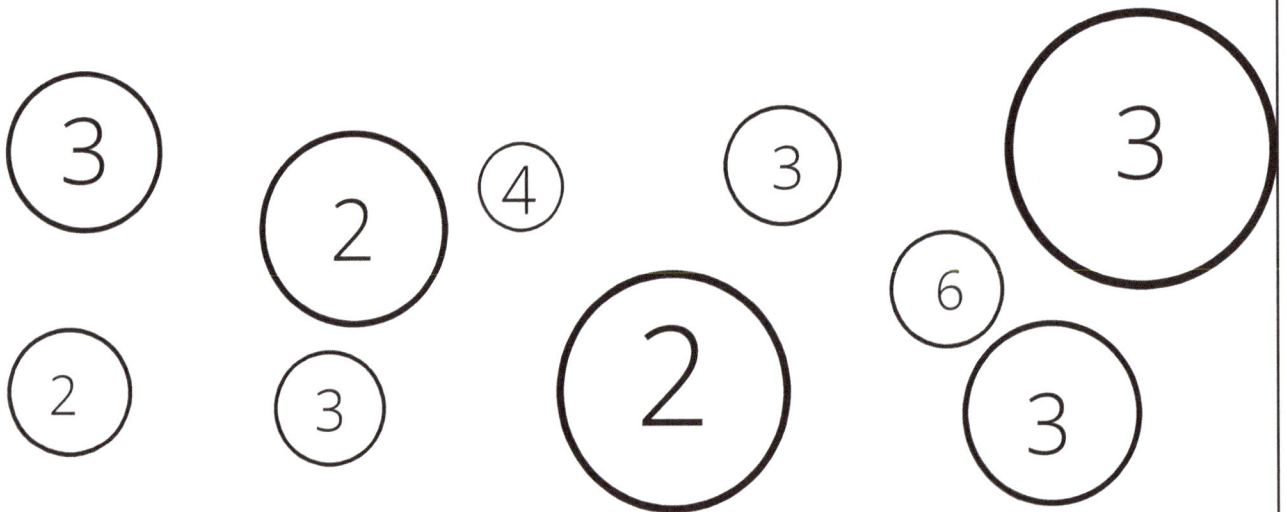

3 2 4 3 3

2 3 2 6 3

Count and color three kites.

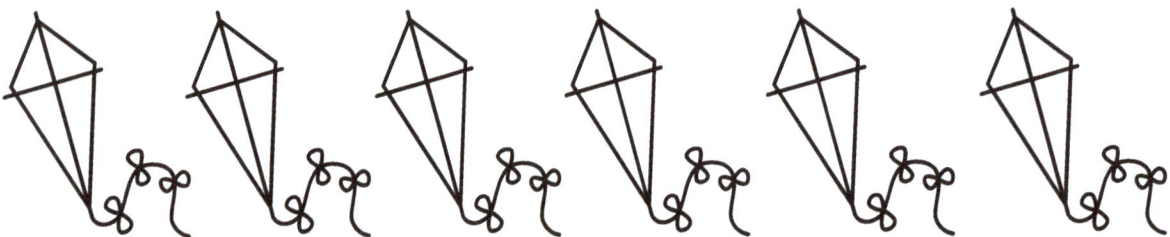

0 1 2 3 4 5 6 7 8 9 10 11 12 13 14 15 16 17 18 19 20 21 22 23 24 25 26 27 28 29 30

4 Four

Color each square with the number 4.

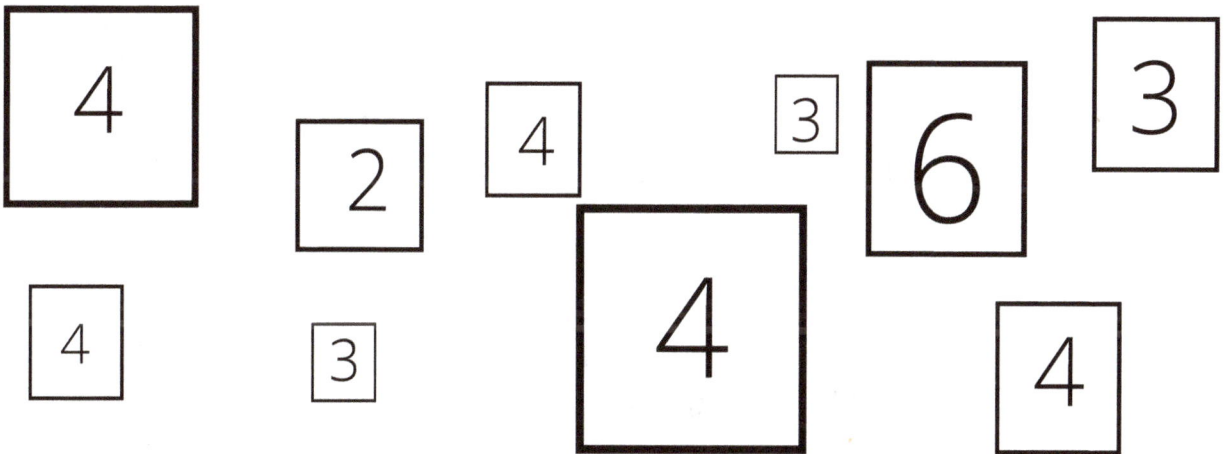

```
4    2    4    3   6    3
4    3        4        4
```

Count and color four dogs.

0 1 2 3 4 5 6 7 8 9 10 11 12 13 14 15 16 17 18 19 20 21 22 23 24 25 26 27 28 29 30

5 Five

Color each triangle with the number 5.

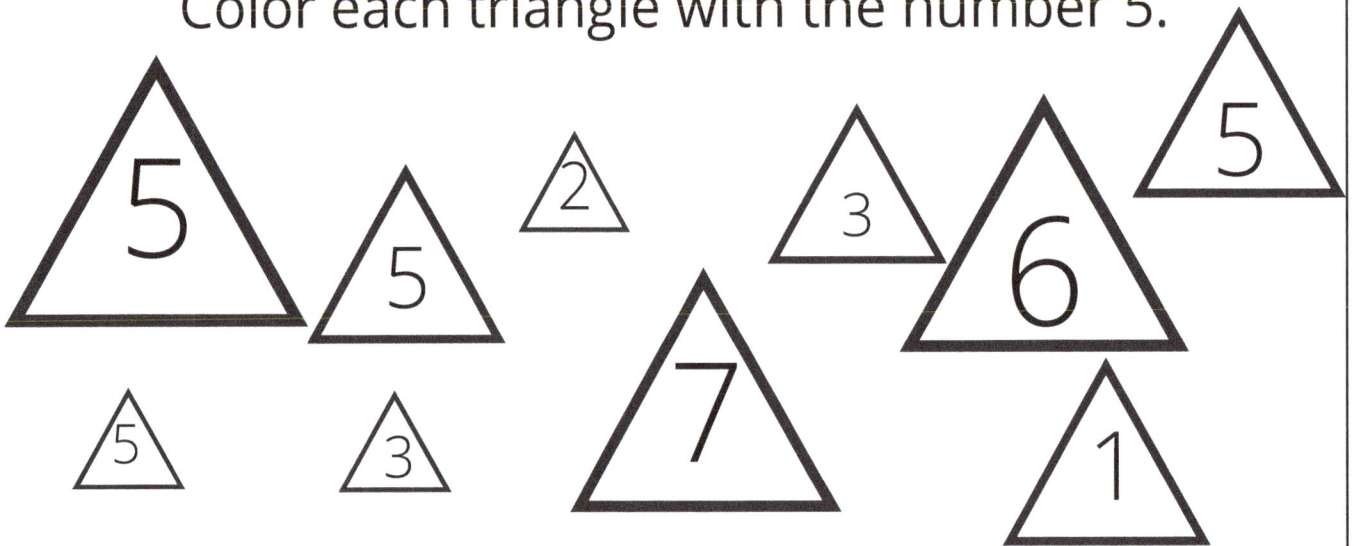

5 5 2 3 5

5 3 7 6 1

Count and color five cats.

0 1 2 3 4 5 6 7 8 9 10 11 12 13 14 15 16 17 18 19 20 21 22 23 24 25 26 27 28 29 30

6 Six

Color each hexagon with the number 6.

6 4 6 3 8

1 6 7 6

6

Count and color six whistles.

0 1 2 3 4 5 6 7 8 9 10 11 12 13 14 15 16 17 18 19 20 21 22 23 24 25 26 27 28 29 30

7 Seven

Color each rhombus with the number 7.

3 5 7 7 7 2 8 1 9 4

Count and color seven bees.

0 1 2 3 4 5 6 7 8 9 10 11 12 13 14 15 16 17 18 19 20 21 22 23 24 25 26 27 28 29 30

8 Eight

Color each octagon with the number 8.

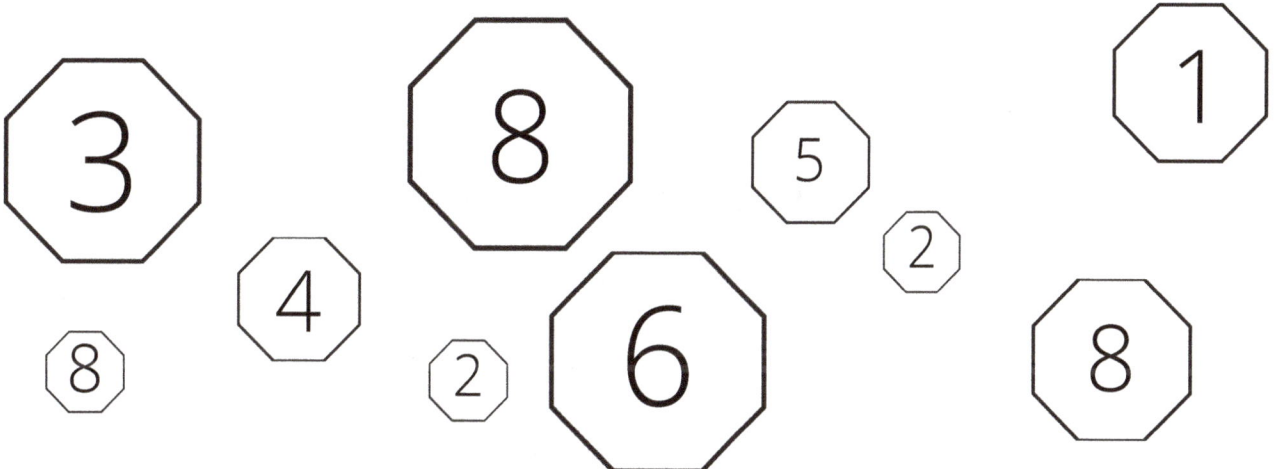

3   8   1

5

4   2

8   2   6   8

Count and color eight footballs.

0 1 2 3 4 5 6 7 8 9 10 11 12 13 14 15 16 17 18 19 20 21 22 23 24 25 26 27 28 29 30

q Nine

Color each oval with the number 8.

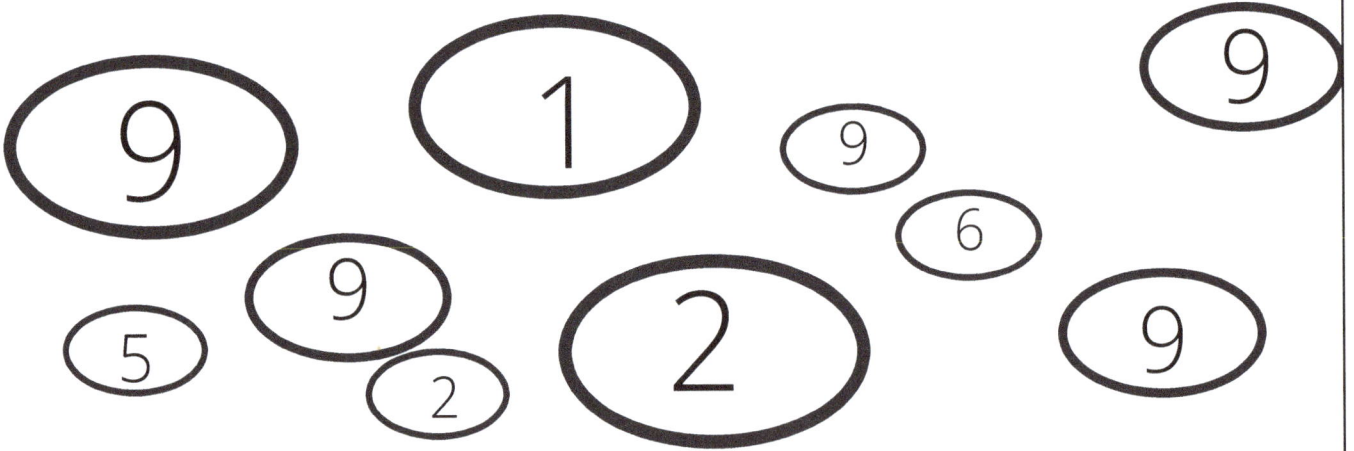

9 1 9 9 9 6 5 9 2 2 9

Count and color nine ice cream cones.

0 1 2 3 4 5 6 7 8 9 10 11 12 13 14 15 16 17 18 19 20 21 22 23 24 25 26 27 28 29 30

10 Ten

Color each raindrop with the number 10.

10 7 2 9 8 10 10 1 10 3

Count and color ten flowers.

0 1 2 3 4 5 6 7 8 9 10 11 12 13 14 15 16 17 18 19 20 21 22 23 24 25 26 27 28 29 30

11 Eleven

Color each parallelogram with the number 11.

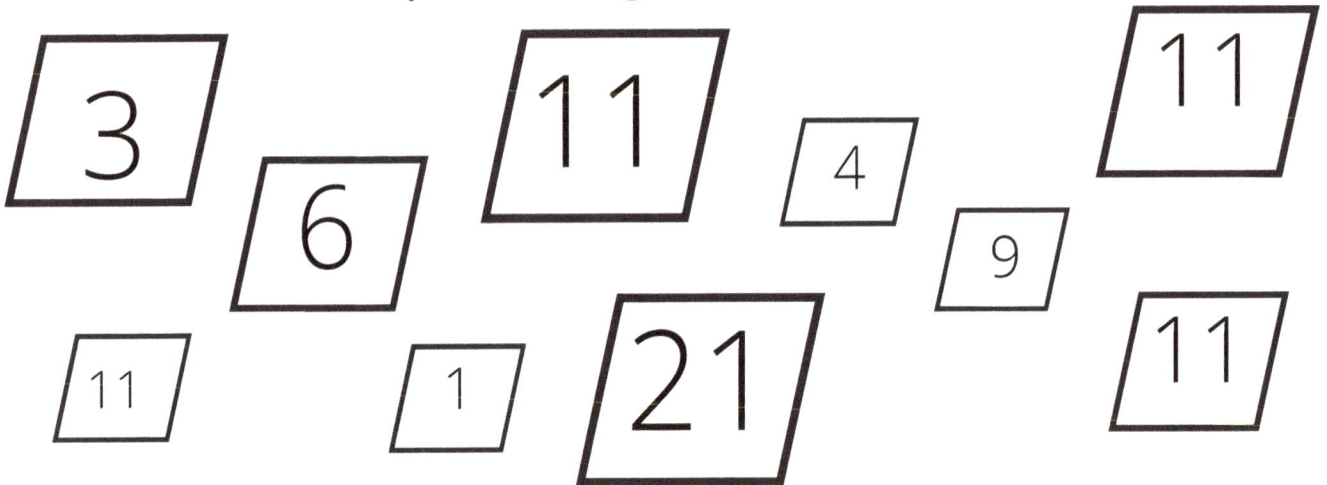

3 11 11

6 4

9

11 1 21 11

Count and color how many in each set.

1.

2.

_____

_____

12 Twelve

Color each sun with the number 12.

12   3   6   9   12

10   12   17   11

Count and color how many in each set.

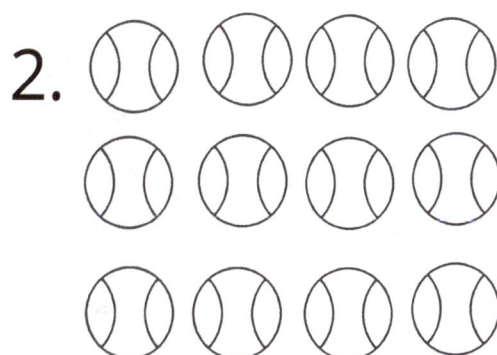

1.   2.

_____   _____

13 Thirteen

Color each pear with the number 13.

Count and color how many in each set.

1.

2.

_____   _____

14 Fourteen

Color each tomato with the number 14.

Count and color how many in each set.

1.

2.

_____   _____

15 Fifteen

Color each lightbulb with the number 15.

5 2 15 13

15 12 15 4 7

Count and color how many in each set.

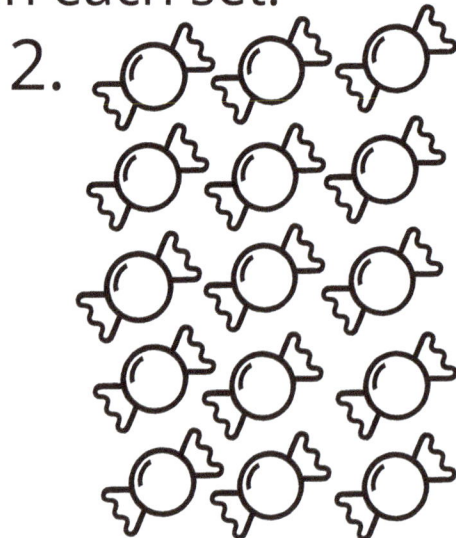

1.

2.

_____   _____

16 Sixteen

Color each mug with the number 16.

16   17   5

61   9   16

10   23   18   16

Count and color how many in each set.

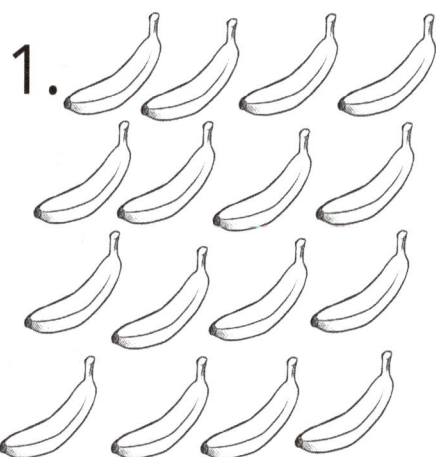

1.

2.

_____   _____

17 Seventeen

Color each coin with the number 17.

Count and color how many in each set.

1.

2.

_____   _____

18 Eighteen

Color each lemon with the number 18.

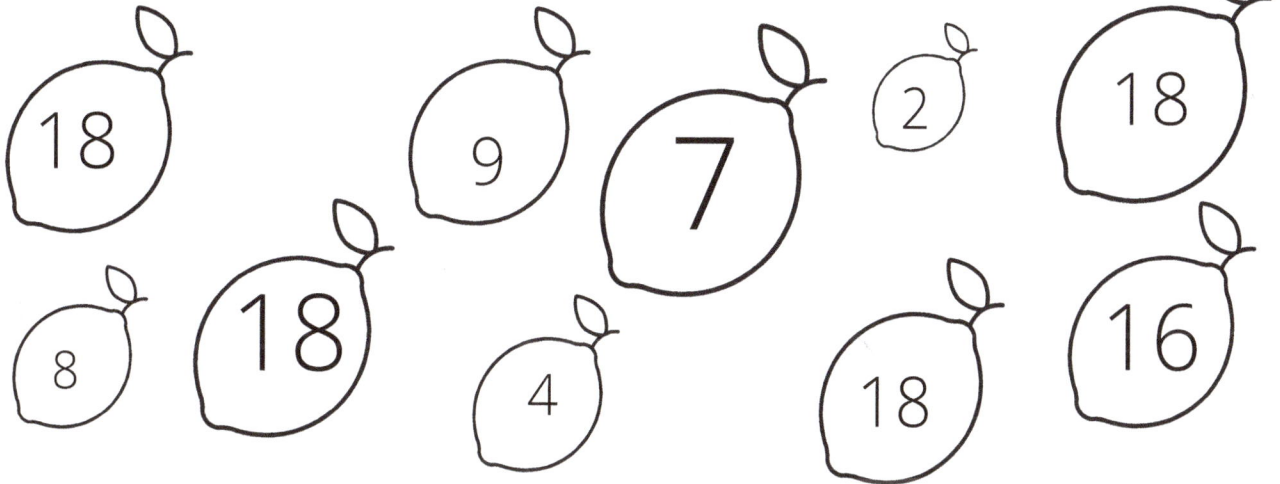

18   9   7   2   18

8   18   4   18   16

Count and color how many in each set.

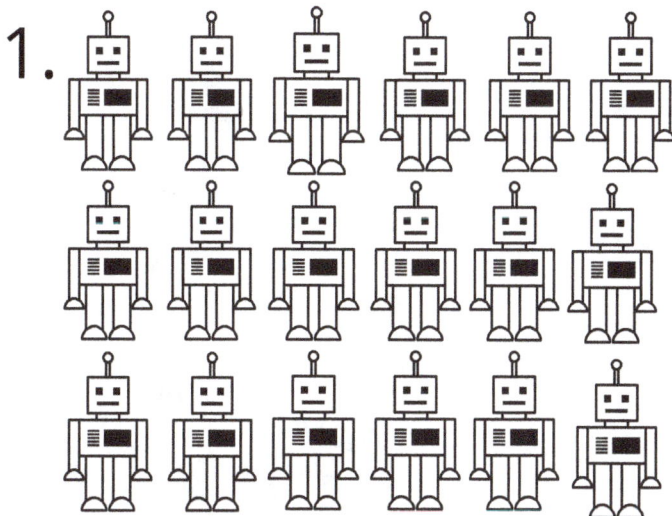

1.

2.

_____   _____

19 Nineteen

Color each truck with the number 19.

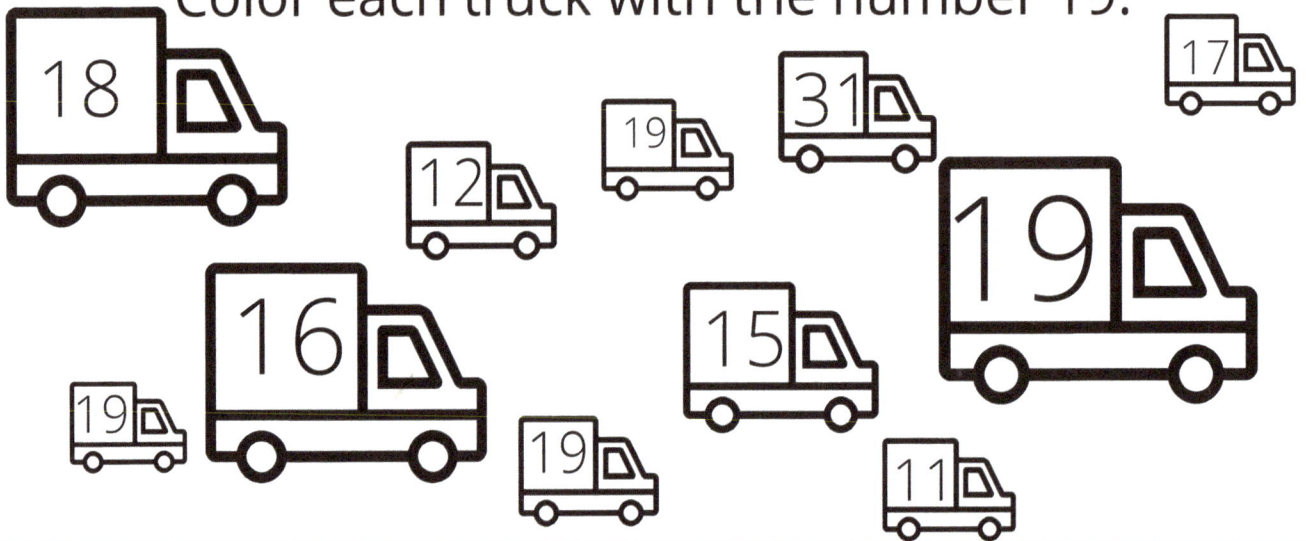

Count and color how many in each set.

1.

2.

_____

_____

20 Twenty

Color each lamp with the number 20.

20 23 17 20 18

02 20 20

14 15 19 20

Count and color how many in each set.

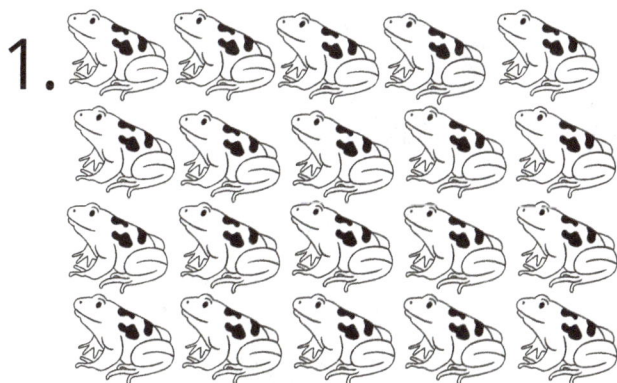

1.

2.

_____ _____

21 Twenty - one

Color each planet with the number 21.

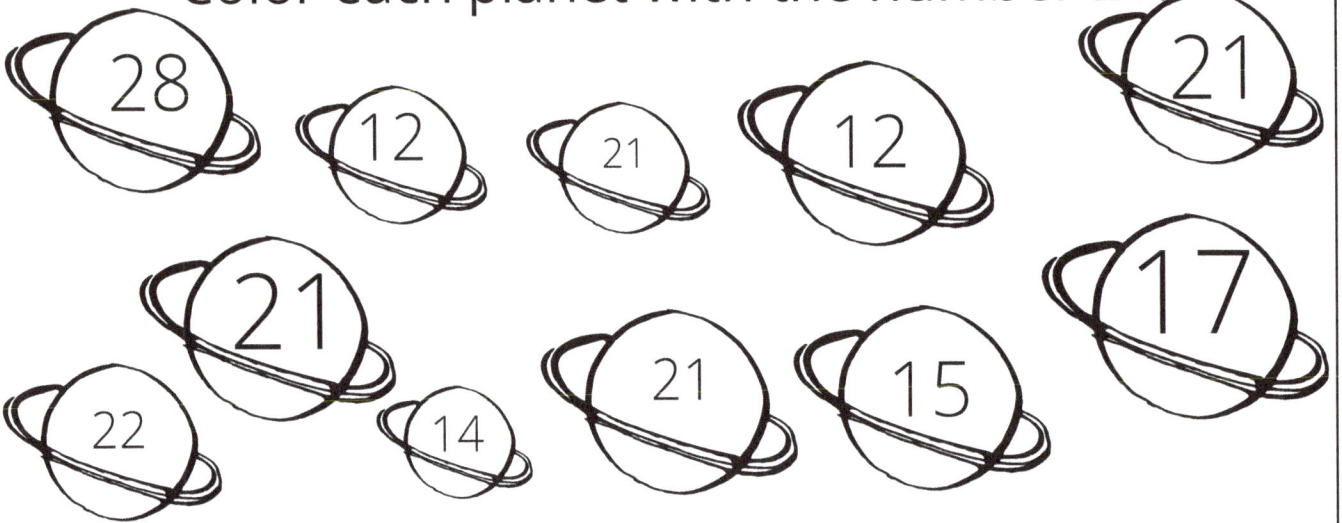

28 12 21 12 21

22 14 21 15 17

Count and color how many in each set.

1.

2.

_____

_____

22 Twenty - two

Color each whale with the number 22

Count and color how many in each set.

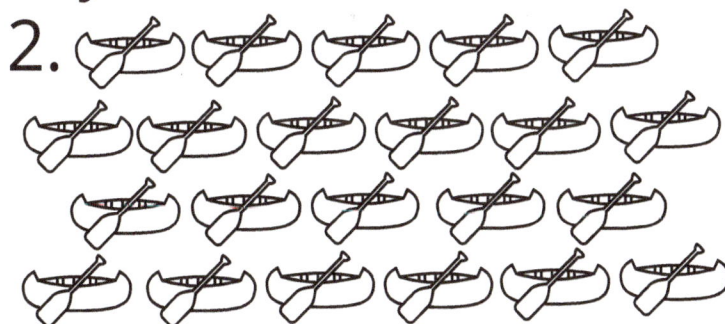

1.

2.

23 Twenty - three

Color each pentagon with the number 23.

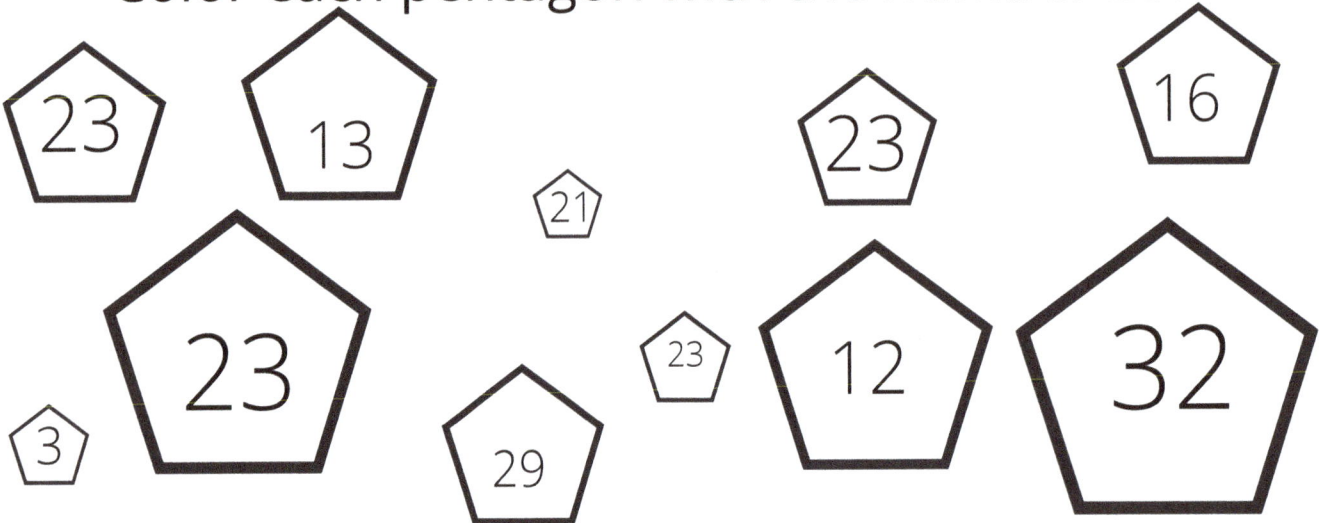

Count and color how many in each set.

1.

2.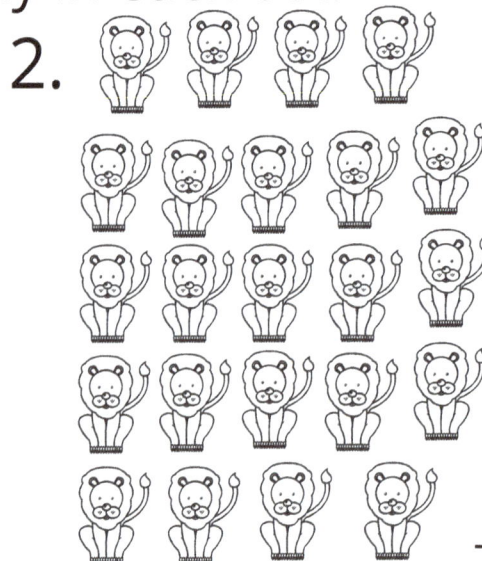

_____

_____

24 Twenty - four

Color each curvilinear triangle with the number 24.

42 28 24 24

12 24 22

24 14 20 16

Count and color how many in each set.

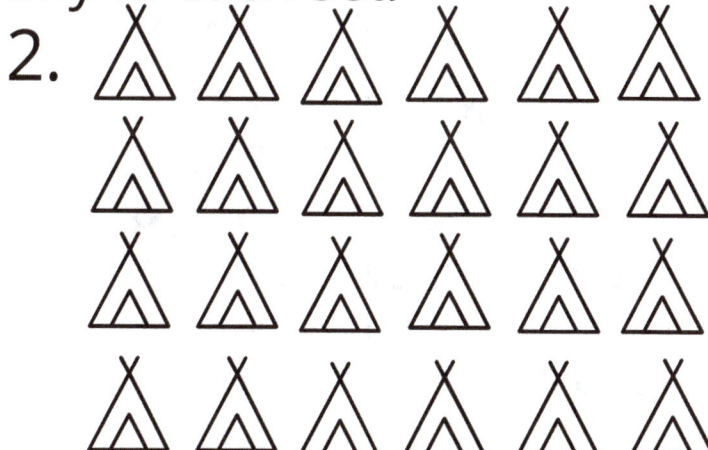

1. 2.

_____   _____

25 Twenty - five

Color each cloud with the number 25.

Count and color how many in each set.

1. 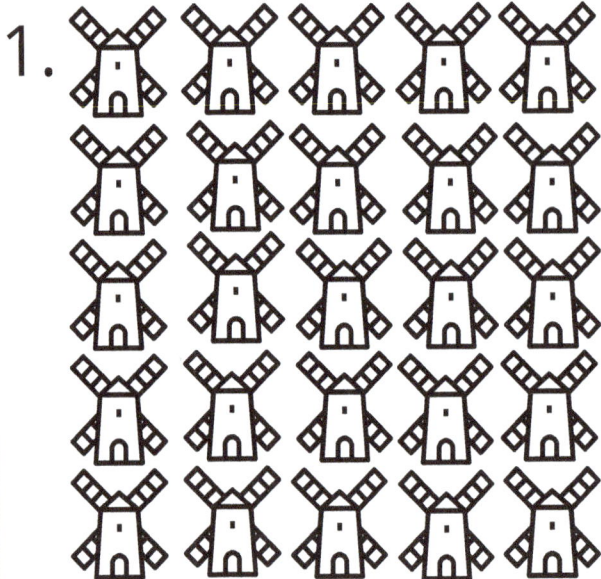 _____

2.  _____

26 Twenty - six

Color each tree with the number 26.

Count and color how many in each set.

1.

2.

_____ _____

27 Twenty - seven

Color each bucket with the number 27.

24 26 17 27 27

27 23 27 23 27

Count and color how many in each set.

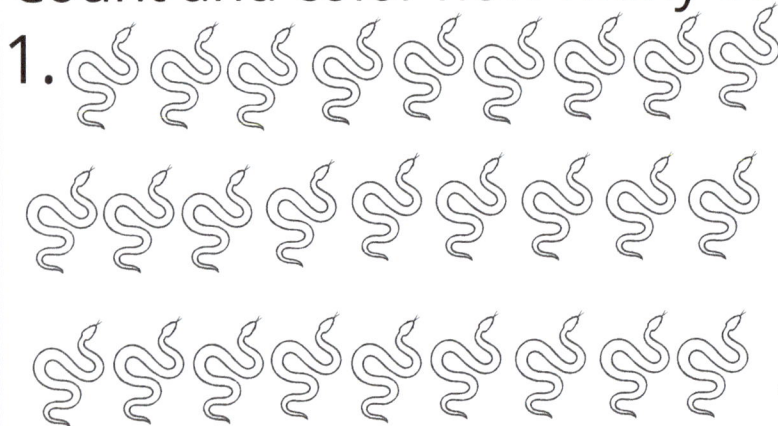

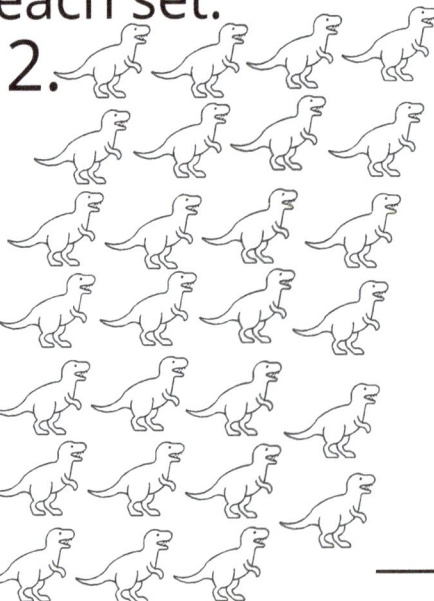

1.

2.

_____   _____

28 Twenty - eight

Color each backpack with the number 28.

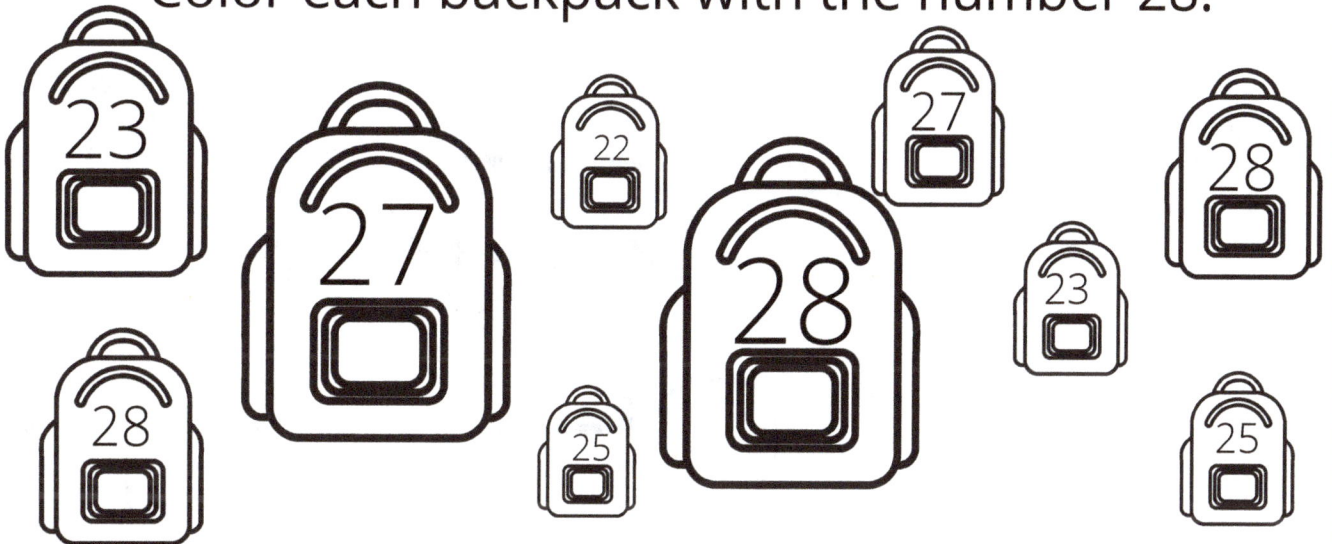

| 23 | 27 | 22 | 27 | 28 |
| 28 | 28 | 25 | 23 | 25 |

Count and color how many in each set.

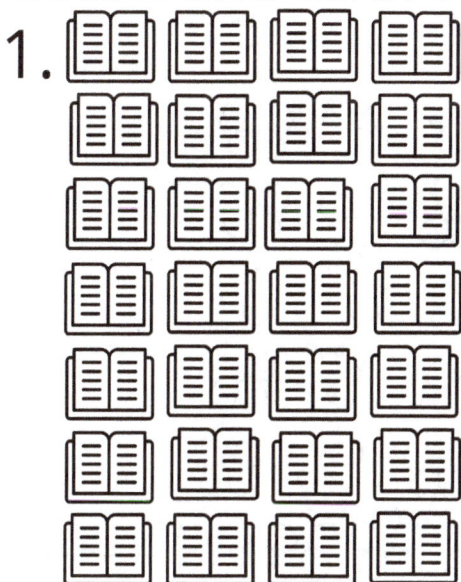

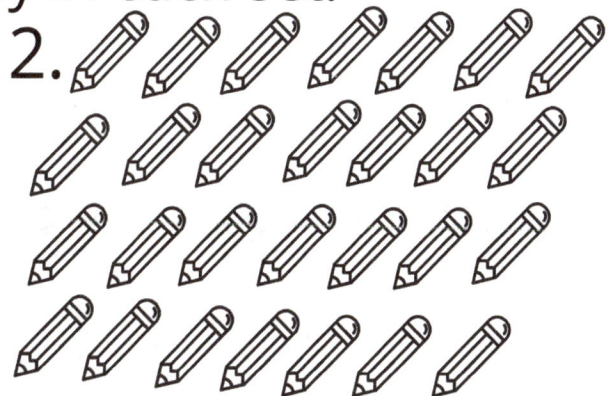

1. _____

2. _____

29 Twenty - nine

Color each shirt with the number 29.

Count and color how many in each set.

1.

2.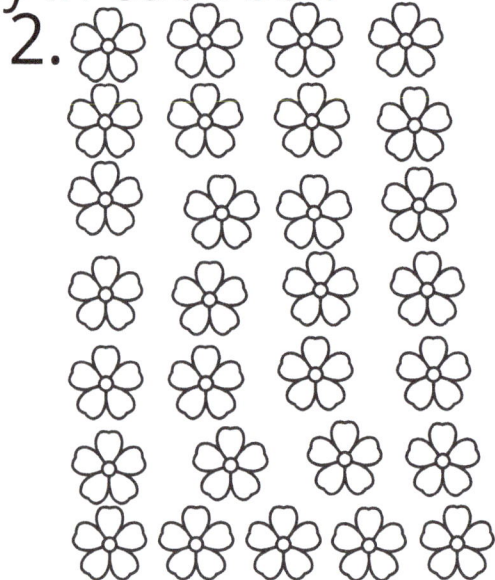

_____   _____

30 Thirty

Color each jar with the number 30.

30

03

30

30

30

30

13

30

27

31

Count and color how many in each set.

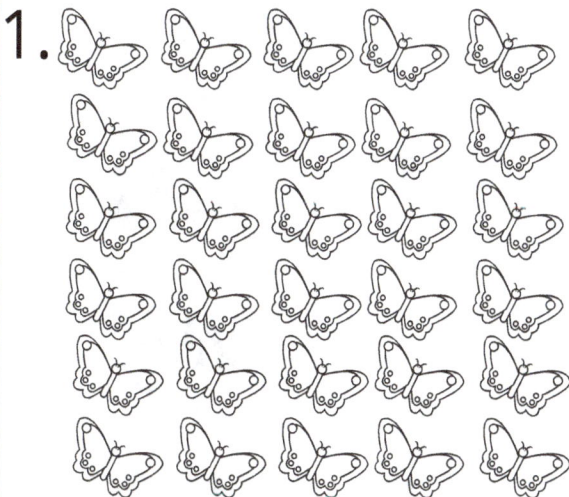

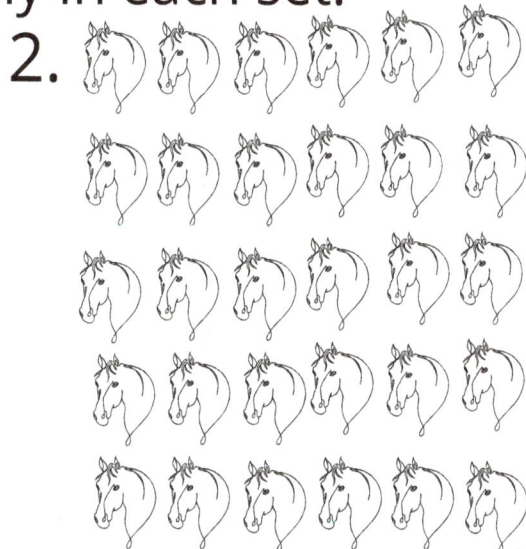

1. _____

2. _____

Numbers 1-50

Practice counting to 50.

1	2	3	4	5
6	7	8	9	10
11	12	13	14	15
16	17	18	19	20
21	22	23	24	25
26	27	28	29	30
31	32	33	34	35
36	37	38	39	40
41	42	43	44	45
46	47	48	49	50

Numbers 1-100

Practice counting to 100.

1	2	3	4	5	6	7	8	9	10
11	12	13	14	15	16	17	18	19	20
21	22	23	24	25	26	27	28	29	30
31	32	33	34	35	36	37	38	39	40
41	42	43	44	45	46	47	48	49	50
51	52	53	54	55	56	57	58	59	60
61	62	63	64	65	66	67	68	69	70
71	72	73	74	75	76	77	78	79	80
81	82	83	84	85	86	87	88	89	90
91	92	93	94	95	96	97	98	99	100

Skip Count By 2

Write the missing number to practice counting by 2's.

1		3		5		7		9	
11		13		15		17		19	
21		23		25		27		29	
31		33		35		37		39	
41		43		45		47		49	
51		53		55		57		59	
61		63		65		67		69	
71		73		75		77		79	
81		83		85		87		89	
91		93		95		97		99	

Skip Count By 5

Write the missing number to practice counting by 5's.

1	2	3	4		6	7	8	9	
11	12	13	14		16	17	18	19	
21	22	23	24		26	27	28	29	
31	32	33	34		36	37	38	39	
41	42	43	44		46	47	48	49	
51	52	53	54		56	57	58	59	
61	62	63	64		66	67	68	69	
71	72	73	74		76	77	78	79	
81	82	83	84		86	87	88	89	
91	92	93	94		96	97	98	99	

Skip Count By 10

Write the missing number to practice counting by 10's.

1	2	3	4	5	6	7	8	9	
11	12	13	14	15	16	17	18	19	
21	22	23	24	25	26	27	28	29	
31	32	33	34	35	36	37	38	39	
41	42	43	44	45	46	47	48	49	
51	52	53	54	55	56	57	58	59	
61	62	63	64	65	66	67	68	69	
71	72	73	74	75	76	77	78	79	
81	82	83	84	85	86	87	88	89	
91	92	93	94	95	96	97	98	99	

Practice counting to 120.

1	2	3	4	5	6	7	8	9	10
11	12	13	14	15	16	17	18	19	20
21	22	23	24	25	26	27	28	29	30
31	32	33	34	35	36	37	38	39	40
41	42	43	44	45	46	47	48	49	50
51	52	53	54	55	56	57	58	59	60
61	62	63	64	65	66	67	68	69	70
71	72	73	74	75	76	77	78	79	80
81	82	83	84	85	86	87	88	89	90
91	92	93	94	95	96	97	98	99	100
101	102	103	104	105	106	107	108	109	110
111	112	113	114	115	116	117	118	119	120

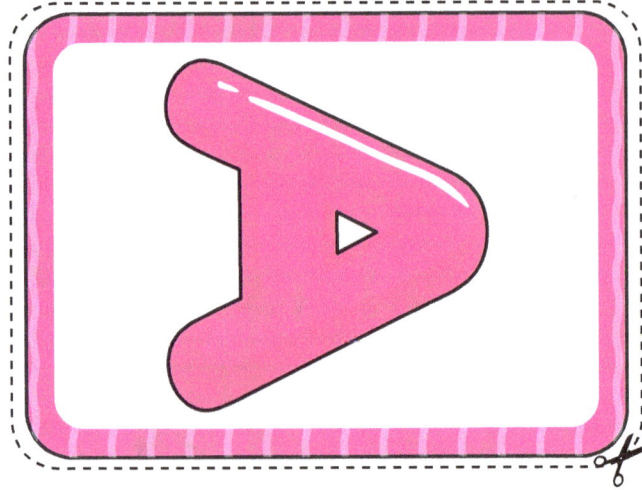

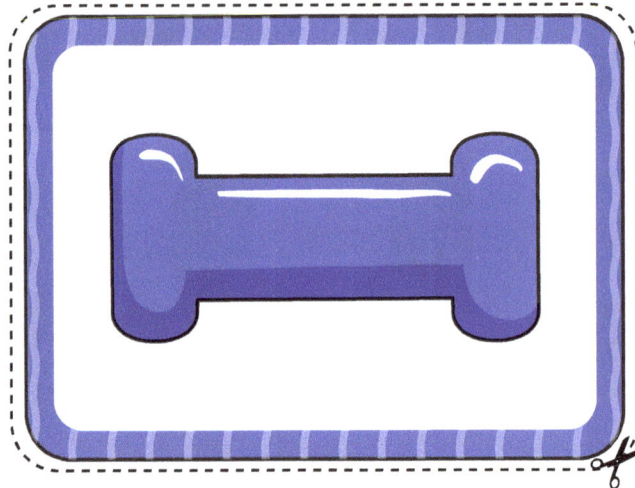

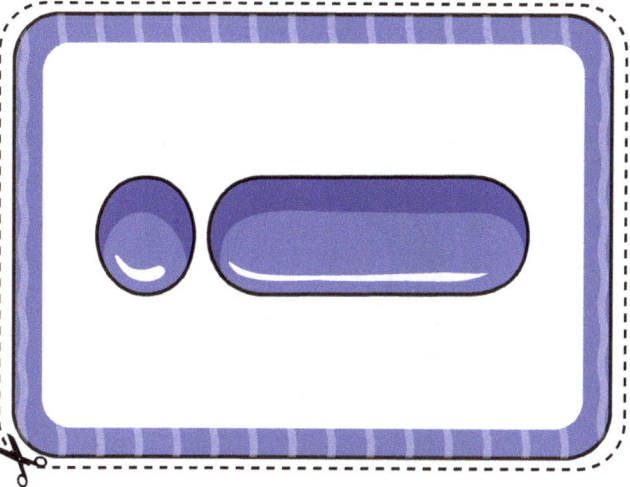

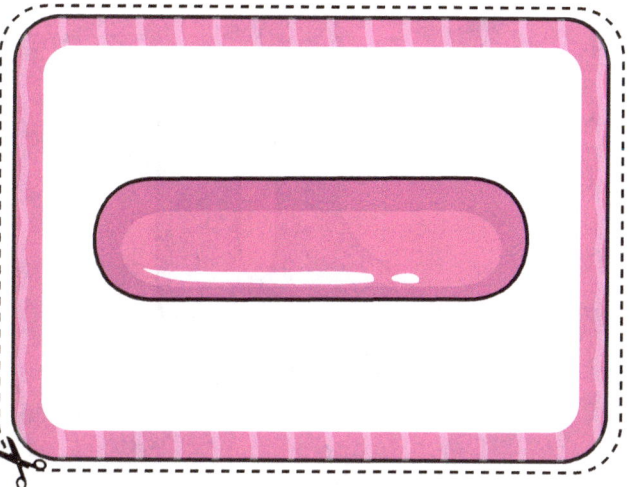

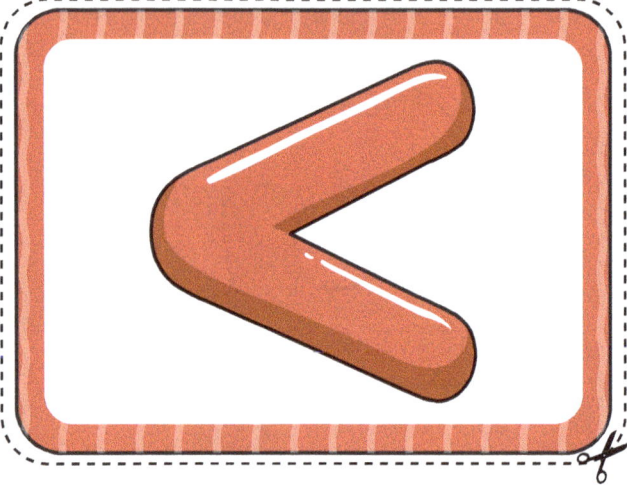

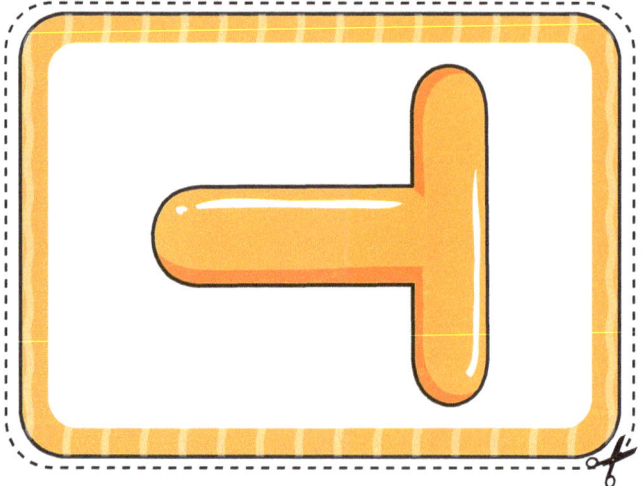

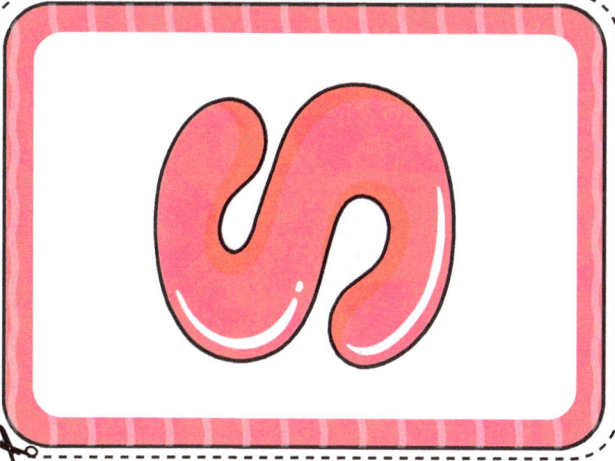

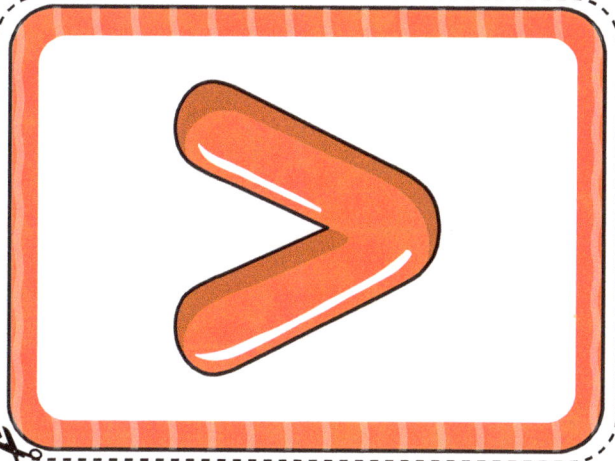

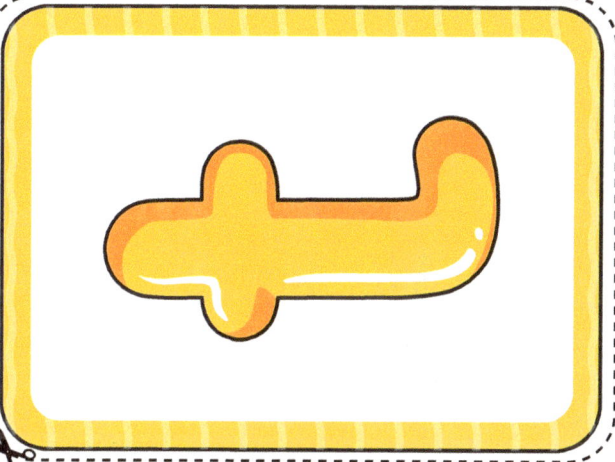

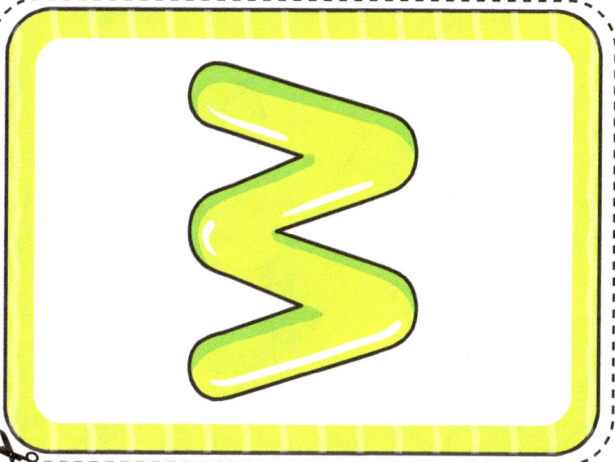

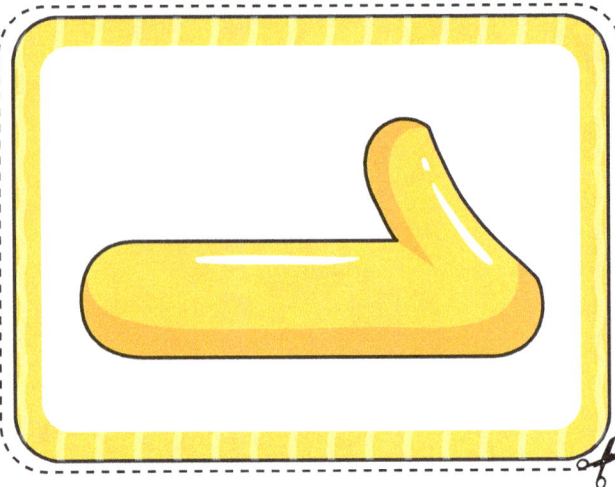

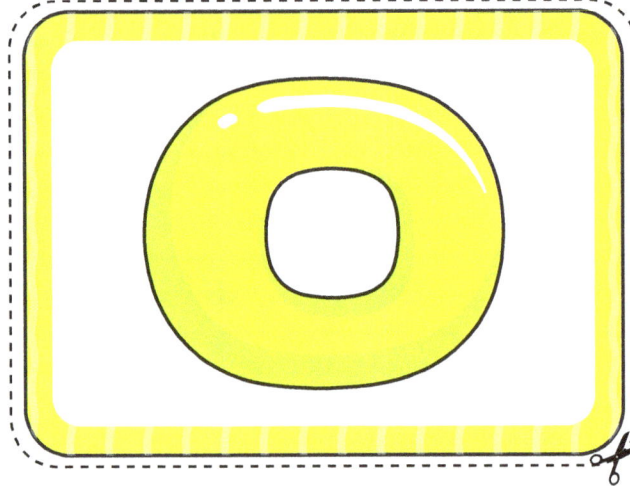

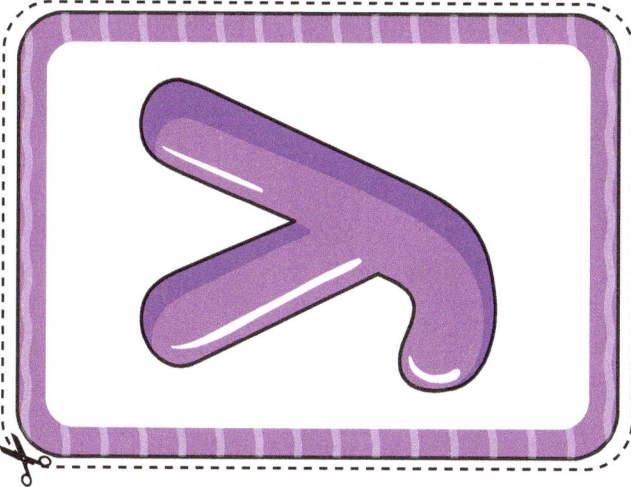

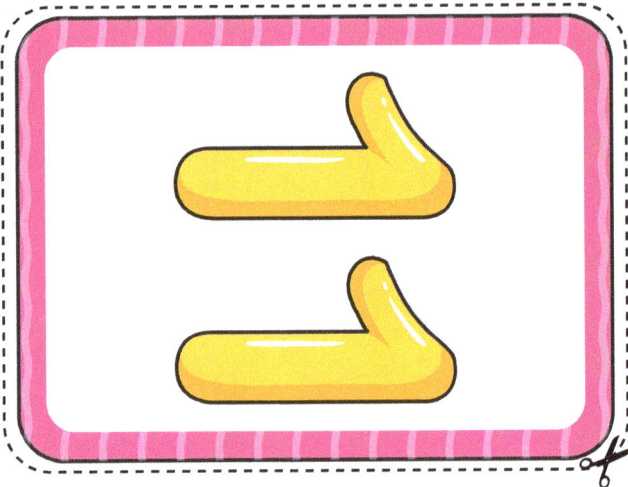

14

17

15

18

16

19

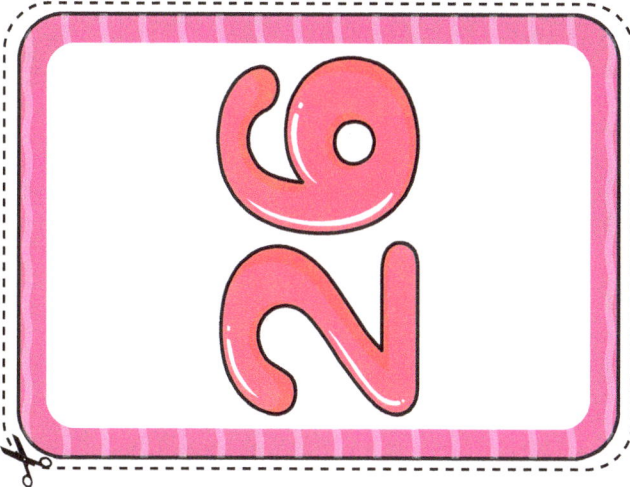

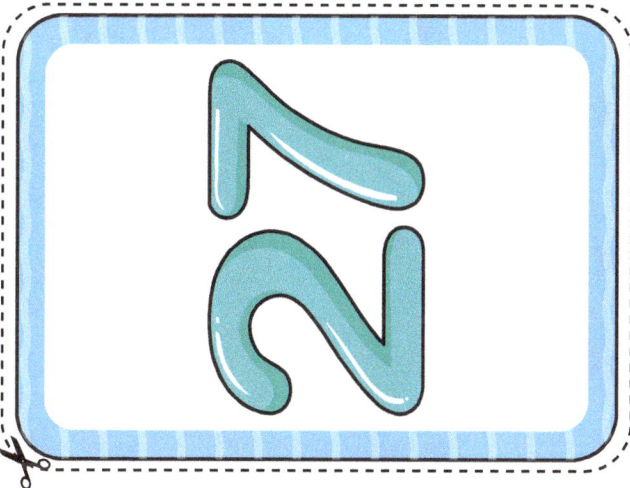

www.ingramcontent.com/pod-product-compliance
Lightning Source LLC
Chambersburg PA
CBHW080419030426
42335CB00020B/2507